DALRIADA

The land that Scotland forgot

BOB JOHNSTON

British Cataloguing in Publication Data
A catalogue record for this book is available from the British Library.

ISBN: 0-9542804-7-4

*

Published in Scotland by Ardminish Press, Isle of Gigha, Argyll. PA41 7AD
www.ardpress.co.uk
E-mail: enquiries@ardpress.co.uk

*

Maps by the author
Cover photographs by Freddy Gillies
Front: Dunaverty, Kintyre: the birthplace of Dalriada
Back: Priceless mediaeval stone carvings at Saddell Abbey

*

£8.99

The author

Bob Johnston is a native of Glasgow, but has lived in Argyll since 1998. He began writing seriously after moving to Campbeltown, and had the award-winning horror story *Life Eternal* published in Volume 17 of the Science Fiction series *Writers of the Future*. This book is his first factual work, but he has long been interested in history and theology, which often feature in his fiction.

Contents

Introduction

Across from the Ardshiel Hotel in Campbeltown, around 50 metres up from the New Quay, is a triangle of grass and trees surrounded by a low stone wall. I had often noticed this area, which has been turned into a small park, complete with benches. A thought that always occurred to me was why nothing had been built on it and why it had been left in such a strange position at several road intersections.

I made enquiries about this strange, but pretty place, and was told that a Dalriadan king was buried there, hence the fact that nothing was built on the site. Further enquiries made it clear that locally there is a belief that this triangle of land is the burial place of King Aedan MacGabrain who ruled Dalriada from 574 until 608.

The information I now had prompted me to dig further, and I was put in contact with Alex McKinven, of Campbeltown, who showed up at my workplace 20 minutes after I had called him; he handed me two books on Argyll history. It was from these first contacts with Alex that this book finally grew, and I have to thank him for his willingness to share his knowledge.

The first confirmed fact was that the king in question was, indeed, Aedan. Dalriada may not be a well-known name among most modern Scots, but King Aedan was one of the most powerful rulers of his day in any part of Britain. The thought that he was buried so close to my home was startling. The second piece of information that Alex verified was that the triangle was not, in fact, the suggested burial site.

It seems that the triangle is located on the site of the Gaelic or Irish Church, which was opened in 1642. Local tradition suggests that this stone built thatched structure was constructed on the site of an existing burial ground. A map of c1750, however, shows the cruciform shape of the Irish Church but there is no indication of a burial ground. It is, therefore, extremely unlikely that there ever was one.

I have to admit that I was not overly dejected. Finding such a powerful legend was still enough to send me looking for more about Dalriada and this book is the result of that search. I am also delighted to say that, in the course of my researches, I established where King Aedan actually is buried, and this is detailed in the book.

The choice of subject matter for each chapter has been quite selective. A book doing full justice to Dalriada, its history and influence on Scotland would run to millions of words. Such a work would have to be scholarly in nature and that is emphatically not what I intend to present here. As far as I have been able, I have confirmed the facts presented. Where I have expressed an opinion of my own I have clearly shown this.

If I have one intention in presenting this work it is to show that Argyll was once an immensely important place, deserving of a much higher profile in the broader history of Scotland and Great Britain than it has received. The extent to which the area has been ignored and neglected by the *official* history of Scotland borders on conspiracy. This was the land that gave us the name 'Scots' but had to find a new identity when the later Scots began to treat the original users of the name as something less than human.

Finally, I dedicate this book to my late grandfather, Tom White, a soldier and avid reader, who, 25 years ago, first told me stories about a place in the west called Dalriada.

BRITAIN
A.D. 847
PICTLAND
DALRIADA
LOTHIAN
STRATHCLYDE
GALLOWAY
BERNICIA
NORTHUMBRIA
DEIRA
0
50
100 km

The destruction of Pictland

In 847 Kenneth MacAlpin, King of the Scots of Dalriada, sent messengers to the nobility of Pictland, inviting them to a feast. From his capital at Dunadd, deep inside Dalriada, these messengers left by several routes. Some crossed the great spine of mountains between the two nations by the southern pass. Others made their way through the northern pass and the remainder took to the ocean that lay within easy sight of Dunadd.

By comparison with Kenneth's Dalriada, Pictland was vast. Both lands combined made up that area which the Romans had named Caledonia, but Dalriada was by far the smaller of the two. It occupied the extreme south west of Caledonia, an area bounded mainly by ocean but in the north-east by difficult mountainous land, that even in the 21st century, can be treacherous and impassable in winter. Pictland occupied the whole vastness of the rest of Caledonia, apart from some territory to the north of the Antonine Wall held for a time by Strathclyde. It was into this vastness that Kenneth's messengers travelled.

The difficulties of travel aside, Kenneth's invitation was in all probability welcomed. The King of the Scots was also a relative of the Picts on his mother's side. Picts had ruled Dalriada in the past and Scots had ruled Pictland. These were two kindred peoples with much mixed blood between them. It must have seemed a tragedy to many, on both sides, that there had been three centuries of occasional, but wasteful, warfare between them.

The Pictish nobles who answered the invitation would also have been conscious of the lamentable state of their kingdom at this time. Only eight years before their aristocracy had been all but wiped out in a great battle against the Vikings at Forteviot. Power had subsequently fallen to the few surviving noblemen and by 847 the Pictish throne was held by Drust MacFerat, a man of undoubted noble blood, but not to be found on any of the genealogies of the day. Such men do not become kings without bringing down the direst of consequences on their people.

We can safely doubt that King Drust attended the feast but many of his nobility will have answered the invitation. Pictland remained under constant threat from the Vikings and it had to be mindful, in its current weakened state, of the two kingdoms to the south. The reality of these kingdoms was that neither was in any serious position to threaten Pictland. Dumnagual IV, who effectively held his throne as a subordinate of the eastern monarch Athelred II, King of Northumbria, ruled Strathclyde, in the west. Although Northumbria enjoyed relative stability, the Vikings also threatened it, and the normal internal strifes prevailed within its frontiers. In 844 Athelred was usurped temporarily by Redwulf, who was subsequently killed halting a Viking raid. With the benefit of hindsight we can see that the Picts had no imminent threats on their southern border. In their depleted state, though, it must have been hard to rely on this and an invite from their cousin, Kenneth, in Dalriada must have seemed like a chance to consolidate, regroup and strengthen an old blood alliance.

Through the long summer days of 847 the Pictish Lords converged on Dunadd from the north, from the east, and from the sea. Dumnagual and his overlord, Athelred, would have received intelligence of the great feast but few, if any, of the Picts would have sought the permission of Strathclyde to pass along the River Clyde and up the long sea lochs to the heart of Dalriada. This was certainly an easier journey, but hardly sensible to goad the suspicions of kings who would already be wondering just what was to happen at Dunadd.

In the space of a few weeks the nobles were gathered and housed at Kenneth's capital. Then, as now, summer can be a fine and beautiful season when the weather remains clement. Indeed, there can be few more beautiful places on earth than the flat valley around Dunadd. Looking to the north-west from the summit of the fort the land spreads out wide and level until it meets the ocean, with the islands of Jura and Scarba beyond. Below the steep cliffs the River Add meanders from the sea and past the fort, providing constant fresh water and a route for boats to be pulled right up to the residence of the king. Indeed, the sea would have come further inland in Kenneth's time. Woodland surrounds the site on all other sides but to the south-east the hills of Cowal can be seen above the trees. Strip away the vegetation and King Kenneth could have seen from shore to shore, across the heart of his realm.

To have any meaningful understanding of what was to follow we have to consider the sort of man Kenneth MacAlpin was, and the times in which he lived. When he sent the invitations to his Pictish cousins Kenneth was in his late 30s. In modern terms this gives him a youthful aspect, but it is clear that by the standards of his time he was well into middle age. It is likely that his adult life began about the age of 14 when he would have been sent away to kinsmen to be trained in the ways of war. Ironically, it is highly likely that these kinsmen were Picts from his mother's line. In fact, most of the Scots boys would have been treated in similar manner, whether they had family across the mountains or not. This policy of the Scots (and we must assume the Picts also) served two purposes. It created young men who were tough, self-reliant and competent fighters. It also took these same young men away at a time in their lives when they were at their most energetic and disruptive. To anyone who has been conscripted for military service this practice will seem very familiar.

Facts about Kenneth's early life are sparse, but it seems likely that he spent very little of it in Dalriada. As well as his time in Pictland he appears to have been connected with family across the North Channel in Ireland. This was the reality of Ireland and Caledonia at this time. Not the Dark Age solitude and intellectual vacuum we are too often asked to accept as representative of this era; rather, a vibrant and busy culture trading with its neighbours as often as it warred with them, taking the sons of its neighbours in as guests as often as it plundered and took slaves. By comparison with the days of Roman control in Britannia there would have been less exotic trade, more turbulence on the southern frontier, but people still lived their lives, grew their crops and traded their goods. Life went on and it would often be good, sometimes terrible. It was just the way life had always been and undoubtedly always will be.

Whether he visited Dalriada or not in his youth he was its king at some time around his 30th year. Some say he had succeeded his father as sub-king of Galloway, an independent Kingdom to the south-west of Strathclyde, said to be kin to the Picts. This is doubtful and may exist only to give Kenneth some royal credentials. In earlier times it would have been important, for without some such tale he appears out of nowhere and swiftly assumes complete control of Dalriada.

So what kind of man emerges from obscurity, assumes an important Royal title, and then goes on to rule successfully and well for 18 years? Clearly only one who could fit in with the prevailing historical forces of the time; a man who could exploit the misfortunes of his neighbours whilst making the most of the strengths of his own people. History paints an image of Kenneth as a mighty, almost Arthurian figure. He comes to us as a strong leader who can wage war with the best of his contemporaries and yet a man who, from these wars, could forge a new kingdom and sow the seeds of future unity among all the peoples of ancient Britannia and Caledonia.

There is no question that Kenneth was a heroic figure, but he was no Arthur. Some sources have him belonging to the Clan Lorne or the Kindred of Lorne, one of the three original Dalriadan tribal groups. This is probably not the case, although the assumption is understandable. The Clan Lorne were Lords of the area in which Dunadd sits. This area, Lorne, at its landward extremities looked across to the Pictish marches and, if Kenneth had Pictish connections, the assumption is that he was more likely from Lorne than from among the southern Clan Gabrain (Kindred of Gabran) or the Clan Oengusa (Kindred of Angus) of Islay. The assumption, though, relies on that Dark Age myth of travel being immensely difficult.

It is altogether more likely that Kenneth was of the Clan Gabrain. This division occupied the southern territories of Dalriada, those closest to the ancient heartland across the water in Ireland. More importantly, the Clan Gabrain held the Overlordship of the Scots and was more likely to furnish Dalriada with a king than the two lesser kin. So Kenneth had the necessary royal blood as well as connections with Ireland and with Pictland. There is also a strong suggestion that his father married again, presumably after the death of Kenneth's mother, to a Viking princess. Kenneth would, then, also have strong links to the Vikings, who were rapidly growing in force throughout the West of Scotland.

So far so good, but, unfortunately for our young *Arthur*, the Scots on both sides of the North Channel kept records. They were as patchy at times as the Anglo-Saxon chronicles of distant Northumbria but in general, just as accurate. From the Irish Annals we find that in 836 Kenneth received a visitor when he was in Dalriada. The purpose of the visit was to discuss the growing problem of Viking attacks on the West Coast, and the visitor was one Gothfrith MacFergus, King of Oriel in Northern Ireland. Gothfrith was of mixed Norse and Pictish blood, and had some degree of control over the southern Hebrides. This bloodline and power base placed him in a very strong position in relation to both Dalriada and Pictland. The fact that he met with Kenneth is also perplexing. At this time both Dalriada and Pictland were regarded as being a joined realm, but the reality was that the kingship was far from settled, and it seems that several claimants either ruled over their own territories or ruled together. The latter option is the most attractive as it simplifies any study of the period but it is difficult to square with the realities of the time. It is daunting enough to serve as a king, beleaguered by external enemies, without wondering if another enemy sits in the adjacent throne.

Whatever the governmental arrangements of the day, Kenneth was not one of the kings of either Dalriada or Pictland. He was, however, in a position to meet with foreign rulers on Dalriadan soil, which tends to confirm his royal credentials. So what was the outcome of this meeting between King Gothfrith of Oriel and the young Prince Kenneth of Dalriada? We have no detailed notes of the meeting but, in the events of the three years following it, one is hard pressed not to see Kenneth moving in the background.

In 839 a Viking army landed in Dalriada and is recorded as advancing through this land into Pictland. The climactic battle took place at Forteviot, where the Pictish nobility were virtually exterminated, leading to the accession of Drust MacFerat. It is worth noting that a considerable number of Scots nobles were also killed at Forteviot alongside their Pictish cousins. There is no doubt that Dalriada and Pictland were still separate kingdoms at this time, but there was a long record of kings from one side or other of the dividing mountains ruling both. Whatever the political situation in 839 the Scots and Picts would have been foolish not to see that they had a common problem with the Vikings. A large number of Scots were clearly not prepared to simply watch the Vikings pass through on their way to Pictland. It is to their eternal credit that they set aside political differences and stood by their cousins at that final, terrible battle.

In the figurative silence that followed the battle, and on into the year 840, chaos reigned. Pictland was the harder hit, being the larger kingdom and having lost more of its leaders. Dalriada, though, had its own burdens to bear. It, too, had lost nobility but there were many princes who felt they had a legitimate claim to the throne. In the background one of their number lay low and bided his time. Kenneth was about to make good on whatever deal he had struck with King Gothfrith of Oriel.

No records have come down to us regarding exactly how Kenneth became king. This is one of those moments in history where the victor may well have taken the opportunity to expunge the relevant chronicles. In modern times this would involve the mammoth task of destroying all pertinent documents. In Kenneth's time it might simply have taken the form of explaining to the scribes of the day that certain events would be best left unrecorded. It is worth noting that, even in our own times, the victor writes the history. It is often enough to simply dictate the focus of that history for the victor to take the moral high ground. To the victorious belong all acts of compassion and chivalry. To the vanquished belong all atrocities and acts of aggression.

To get any feel for Kenneth's possible route to power we will return in due course to his great feast at Dunadd. For the moment we must concentrate on the devastated kingdom he inherited from his predecessor. The records show that the Vikings passed through Dalriada, and it would be foolish to think that they did not cause some measure of destruction at that time. Their aim, though, was the larger kingdom beyond the mountains. That there were Scots nobles already on the other side of these mountains suggests that both kingdoms had made careful plans for this attack. The Scots clearly knew that they could not stop the Viking menace within Dalriada. Any such attempt would simply have given the Vikings some battle practice before crossing the mountains. The sensible option had been taken to withdraw all fighting men into Pictland, and there engage the enemy with the largest possible combined force. That it failed does not mean it was not the best available plan. The Vikings were simply too strong for the defending army.

After Forteviot we find only chaos. The Vikings were satisfied with the destruction of the Pictish nobility and they made no effort to hold control of the kingdom. Kenneth moved swiftly, but cautiously, to secure his position. In the years immediately following Forteviot he assumed the Kingship of Dalriada, but Pictland was left to recover as best it could. This fits with the picture of Kenneth. Any immediate move on Pictland would probably have been a disaster. It would have demonstrated some measure of collusion with the Vikings and it would have overstretched his efforts. His position in Dalriada was by no means secure in the early years and attempting to press a claim to two thrones would have been foolish and quite out of keeping with the careful and cunning personality that was serving Kenneth so well up till now. He first strengthened his hold on Dalriada and, only when the time was right, turned his attentions to the east.

The time was clearly appropriate when Kenneth arranged his great feast. After some years consolidating and securing his realm, he now felt able to turn his attentions back to Pictland. The view of the two nations on either side of the mountains must have been quite different. Dalriada had enjoyed nearly a decade of admittedly wary security while Pictland had struggled to find any degree of order. After Forteviot in 839 the throne of Pictland was quickly filled by a surviving Earl, Ferat son of Bargoit. In 842 Ferat rather conveniently died just as Kenneth was casting his attentions eastwards again. Again, it is increasingly easy to see Kenneth's hand in such events. Was he ready to assume control after Ferat's death? He may not have had any concrete plans to do so, but the expedient of having the rival king removed would give him a very clear picture of the internal condition of Pictland.

As it was, Ferat's son, Brude, immediately claimed his father's throne. Mere weeks later Brude was dead and his brother, Kineth, was king. A year later Kineth was gone, dead or deposed, and one Brude MacFochel had assumed the shaky purple. Two years later Brude was gone. He held power for two short years, and we can assume that he had acquired the sense and survival instinct to flee at the end. The histories have him deposed rather than killed. After Brude came Ferat's youngest son Drust, whom we have already met.

If we compare the kings, we see in Pictland the youngest son of an earl finally taking power after several years of destructive infighting. In Dalriada we see a prince of royal blood taking power and carefully building his country back to strength. Obviously this view has to taken carefully. It was Kenneth, after all, who got to write the final version of history. In terms of the relative stability of the kingdoms, though, the comparison is at least figuratively correct.

This may be a good point to pause and consider Kenneth's lineage in a little more detail. History has been kind to him and his successes account for a good part of this. Indeed a purpose of this book is to record his achievements and their subsequent importance to Great Britain. From the preceding narrative we can glean a small picture of the type of man he was. That he had greatness in him is beyond doubt, but greatness is a trait found as often in peasants as in great lords, as often in ordinary soldiers as in their generals. Unfortunately it has always been harder for the peasant and the soldier to let their greatness shine forth. In essence, Kenneth could assume the Kingship of Dalriada with no lineage at all. Hadn't Ferat, Brude, Kineth, the other Brude and finally Drust done just that in Pictland? Of course they had, but in the chaos they inherited they had nothing to rally their people to. They were not of the royal line and, whilst they could undoubtedly rely on the support of the fighting men of their own lands, they had nothing to attract the loyalty of the men of other lords.

In Dalriada the situation was broadly the same. Any nobleman would have endless difficulties trying to rally the people of areas over which he had no inherited authority. This would present a difficulty to Kenneth, a prince of the Clan Gabrain, in his dealings with the Clan Lorne and the Clan Oengusa.. He would, however, have an advantage that the Pictish Earls did not. The Clan Gabrain held the Overlordship of Dalriada. If Kenneth could convincingly prove that he had an acceptable lineage within this kindred then his ascent to the throne would be considerably smoother than that of his hapless counterparts in Pictland.

Kenneth started from a good position. He was undoubtedly of royal blood but his low profile in the years before 839 is a clear indication that he was a very junior member of his kin. For a distant royal cousin to become King was far from impossible. Getting the throne seems to have been perfectly within the capacities of many. Keeping it, as Ferat, Brude, Kineth, Brude and Drust had discovered across the mountains, was altogether trickier. To secure his position Kenneth had to present a strong and acceptable lineage.

The documents of the age are remarkable in their accuracy, whether we are referring to the Annals of Ulster or the Anglo-Saxon Chronicles. Where they suffer, it is not in the accuracy of their contents but in the selective nature of the entries. Unfortunately the lineages of the day served different purposes. They existed to support family claims to territory, to titles and, indeed, to illustrious forebears. Often the compilers of these lineages were not averse to inserting fictitious persons and ascribing to these all manner of claims to fame. Undoubtedly these insertions were based on real people. Two or more might be conjoined under one name, kings might be removed from their own time and placed many years before or after to fit an inconvenient gap and the deeds of great un-named generals would be collected, updated and given to another leader – real or created.

That this could occur should not really seem odd to us. In the current age the compilation of family trees is a thriving business, particularly in the New World. For a payment it is remarkable how often a family tree shows a close link to European Royalty. Perhaps this is a genuine result of the tree narrowing as we run backwards through time. Perhaps it is the result of selectively focusing on only certain bloodlines. This, after all, was one of the expedients England's Henry V resorted to when he presented a claim to the French throne. And perhaps it is the result of giving the paying client what that client wants. However it is, a look at Kenneth's lineage presents us with some interesting characters.

Kenneth's surname clearly indicates that he was the son of Alpin, and a search of the genealogies does uncover an Alpin who ruled Galloway in 834. From the steep hills along the Clyde coast of Kintyre Galloway can be seen to the far south-east, but politically it and Dalriada might as well have been worlds apart in 834. The country was nothing more than a sub-kingdom of Strathclyde which itself had been ruled by Northumbria for generations. The importance of this Alpin is not what he was but rather whom he was descended from. The genealogy has him being the son of Eochaid and the grandson of Aed Find. We will return to Eochaid but Aed Find deserves more immediate attention.

In the years preceding 750 the picture of northern Britain was dramatically different from that of Kenneth's time nearly a century later. Northumbria was just returning to its former glory, but was regularly beset by difficulties. In part these allowed the Pictish King, Angus MacFergus, to consolidate his own power over not only Pictland and Dalriada, but also Strathclyde, probably as Overlord rather than King. For many years then, Angus ruled a territory that was in great part what would later be called Scotland. Tempting as it is to see him as some proto-King of Scots, his kingship was never firmly established as such and, although he was for a time the most powerful ruler in the island of Britain, his reign never managed to bring any sense of unity to his peoples. They remained what they had always been – The Scots in Dalriada, the Picts in Pictland, the Britons in Strathclyde; revolt was only a matter of time.

It is also tempting to see in Angus another latter day Arthur, but again Angus was a man and a leader of his times. The Irish Annals are full of accounts of his triumphs, precisely what we would expect of so powerful a king. Sometimes, though, the annals of the enemy can hint at the true nature of the man. A Saxon chronicler states with admirable simplicity: 'he was a bloody tyrant throughout his whole reign'. His apparent disinterest in assuming the kingships of occupied territories might also suggest a measure of humility. But in reality, when all is weighed up, it comes over as straightforward empire building. In temperament he seems more like a future English King, Edward I. What use are many great and petty titles when the reality is that you are overlord of everything you touch.

If he was not admirable he was at least effective and not given to indecision. In 733, one Prince Dungal of Dalriada seized Angus's son from Toraic (now Tory) Island off the North Coast of Ireland. In the process of taking Prince Bruidhi, a sanctuary was desecrated. The Annals of Ulster and the Annals of Tigernach provide some detail of the results of this ill-considered assault but a brief resume will suffice to show the sort of man Angus was.

In 734 Angus invaded Dalriada. He took Dunolly, near Oban, and seized an exile from his own country in the process, Talorgan the Mormaor of Atholl. He then destroyed Dungal's fort at Dunleven, but missed Dungal who fled to Ireland. Unfortunately the lack of good sense that had prompted him to seize Bruidhi in the first place now sent Dungal back to Dalriada. At Dunadd Angus finally caught the man who had assaulted his son. It is probably best not to consider what Angus did to Dungal, but in 736 at the Battle of Knock Cairpre near Loch Linnhe, he brought the Clan Lorne (Dungal's family) to utter ruin. This ancient family of the Scots never again appears as a separate power. Angus had swiftly avenged the outrage against his son who had died as a result of harsh treatment at the hands of Dungal.

In 750 Strathclyde rebelled. At the same time Aed Find took his chance and took control in Dalriada. Overcome by difficulties, Angus was unable to prevent either kingdom from throwing off his rule. Strathclyde's triumphant bid for freedom was, sadly, short-lived. Within six years the Britons were subjects of Northumbria, and would remain so for the next century. Dalriada fared better, but Angus finally rallied his still formidable strength and for the rest of his reign there was no permanent peace between the two lands. Full-scale war seems to have been avoided for a considerable number of years, but we must assume that Angus was of no mind to accept Dalriada's independence. For as long as this battered but still powerful Pictish King refused to treat with Aed as an equal, war was inevitable.

When the war finally erupted it was swift and decisive. It also came seven years after Angus died. In 768 Ciniod MacFeredach, who appears to have treated Dalriada as still a subject nation, held the Pictish throne. We have to assume from this attitude that Aed Find's kingship was far from secure. Faced with an ongoing claim by the Pictish King and an obstinate refusal to accept that Dalriada was now a sovereign realm, Aed was finally faced with the inescapable conclusion that only arms could decide the issue. In that year of 768 he took the battle into Pictland.

No details of Aed's attack on Ciniod have been recorded, but from 768 onwards Dalriada was no longer harassed by the claims of Pictish Kings. Indeed the Pictish Kings from then on enter a period of long decline. It is safe to assume that Aed succeeded in impressing on the Picts that Dalriada had become a force to be reckoned with.

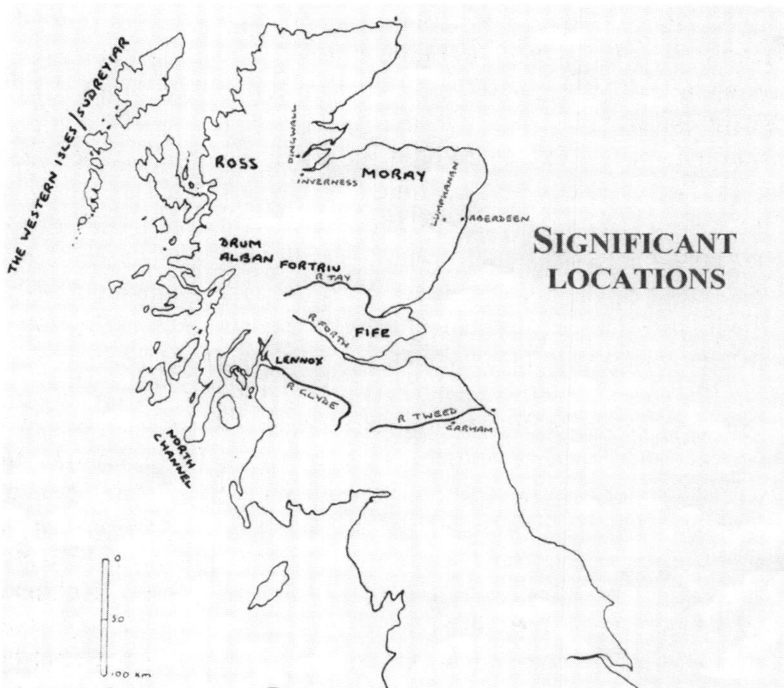
SIGNIFICANT LOCATIONS
THE WESTERN ISLES/SUDREYIAR
ROSS
DINGWALL
INVERNESS
MORAY
LUMPHANAN
ABERDEEN
DRUM ALBAN
FORTRIU
R TAY
R FORTH
FIFE
LENNOX
R CLYDE
R TWEED
CARHAM
NORTH CHANNEL
0
50
100 km

So, in the 18th year of his reign, King Aed Find finally secured Dalriada. For all the claims of Angus and his successors the whole period of Aed's rule is marked by relative peace and stability. From his clash with the Picts at Fortriu in 768 Aed set about governing his kingdom with wisdom and foresight. He established a set of laws, which would in time be adopted throughout what would be Albany. For this, and doubtless many other inspirational acts, Aed well deserves his nickname *The Fair.* Following his death in 778 there were instances of Pictish Kings ruling Dalriada, but never again as conquerors – always by some legitimate succession. If this man was indeed Kenneth MacAlpin's great-grandfather then Kenneth had a truly noble heritage.

Aed Find is recorded as having a son named Eochaid. This Eochaid IV presents many difficulties when attempting to establish Kenneth MacAlpin's lineage. The length of his rule is vague and appears to coincide with that of other shadowy kings, Domnall and Donncorci. This was a period of escalating Viking raids yet there is little in the way of records to show how Dalriada survived and who led it through these difficult times. It may have been that the then Pictish King Constantine had established control over Dalriada, and had appointed leaders to the various parts of that kingdom. If this was the case then that control may well have been assumed unwillingly and certainly with no intention of becoming king in the long term. Interestingly, Constantine was the son of a Dalriadan King which may have influenced his involvement in its troubled affairs.

It is not unreasonable to accept that Eochaid was an appointed sub-king, but the dates make it extremely unlikely that he could have lived long enough to pass the kingdom to his son, Alpin, the father of Kenneth. He is, however, well placed to be considered as the source of the legendary Achaius, who established relations with Emperor Charlemagne. As Charlemagne was King of the Franks this relationship is regarded as the mythical source of the long alliance between the Scots and the French, the *Auld Alliance*. This Achaius is also regarded as the originator of the Order of the Thistle.

It cannot be safely affirmed that Eochaid IV ever existed. There were undoubtedly rulers of Dalriada at this time but it is precisely the dangers of the time and the exploits of Achaius that speak against Eochaid. Any man who helped Dalriada survive through the Viking raids, who spoke with the founder of the Holy Roman Empire, and who established a noble order that survives to this day would be more clearly remembered. Aed Find, his alleged father, never had such exploits yet he is remembered well by history. This may well have been one of those moments when a leader was needed, with a certain name and living to fulfil specific historical events. So Eochaid, who was Achaius, was king at the time that Charlemagne was crowned Emperor by the Pope, in the year 800. One thing this shadowy and doubtful king does prove is that the Picts and the Scots had an eye on the world at large, at a time which is too often described as a Dark Age.

We now return to Kenneth MacAlpin and have to conclude that his lineage from Aed Find is suspect. Whoever his grandfather and father were they were probably not Eochaid and Alpin, who may not even have existed. That he was of royal blood we cannot doubt; this would have given him access to the seats of power. That he was politically astute and appropriately connected we can assume from his meeting with the King of Oriel. From all the facts that can be found, and from the conclusions that can be drawn, there is little doubt that, after the Viking advance through Dalriada in 839, there was not a nobleman in Dalriada better placed than Kenneth to become King.

Did Kenneth have the chroniclers of the day invent Eochaid and Alpin after his accession to validate his kingship? Such an order has all the hallmarks of a shrewd and careful ruler. It does, however, also suggest the calculating ruthlessness of a man who was prepared to do anything to further his own cause. The events at Dunadd in 847 would put the final seal on the character of this man. At Kenneth's stronghold, in the centre of Crinan Moss and, under the long twilit night skies of the Dalriadan summer, the King of the Scots would, once and for all, settle the relationship between the Scots and Picts.

It is tempting to imagine the great feast at Dunadd being some riotous affair along the lines of legendary Anglo-Saxon gatherings. It certainly would not have been to the delicate tastes of modern Scots, but there would have been some degree of protocol. This was a royal court after all. Tables would have been set according to a pecking order, and the Pictish Lords would have sat apart from their Dalriadan counterparts. There would also have been no weapons in the feasting hall.

As the food arrived and the wine and beer flowed, the atmosphere must have livened up marvellously. With Kenneth at the head of the proceedings the Picts and Scots would have exchanged news of their intricately connected families. Some may have fought side by side at Forteviot eight years earlier, and old soldiers are notorious spinners of yarns and recounters of heroics. We can imagine a noisy but friendly gathering stretching into the night, with the Picts becoming increasingly drunk and incapable.

At the opposite tables the Scots may have looked every bit as drunk as their guests, but it is doubtful a drop of real drink had passed their lips all night. At a secret sign from Kenneth, servants quietly moved to positions behind the Pictish benches. These had been specially constructed to collapse backwards and were only held up by concealed bolts. When Kenneth was certain that his warriors were ready he made the sign for the bolts to be hauled out.

As the Scots stormed over their own tables, hidden weapons now in their hands, the Picts fell backwards. Behind them the solid earth floor turned out to be a long camouflaged pit covered over and cleverly concealed. Drunk, shocked and scrambling over one another in the pit the Picts were quickly hacked to pieces by the Scots warriors. None would have had a chance to defend themselves.

As the stench of blood and viscera overwhelmed the smells of food and drink Kenneth calmly observed the result of this penultimate act of deceit and treachery. Penultimate, because it now only remained to move on the leaderless Pictland and take it once and for all. In the coming months the Scots swept across the mountains and crushed what little opposition remained. With the demise of its last lords Pictland was broken and absorbed into the Kingdom of the Scots.

A disgraceful betrayal and a sickening way for Scotland to be born but, fortunately, the great feast described above never took place. The subsequent invasion and ruin of Pictland is also pure myth. The stories do, however, have a certain validity and usefulness. Kenneth *did* take Pictland and he *did* secure the Kingship of Dalriada by deceit and guile. As has been observed before, history has been kind to Kenneth. He deserves praise for his successes and for the foundations he laid but, any time we are tempted to make a saint of this *Arthur*, we should remember the great feast at Dunadd. It never took place but it is precisely the sort of measure King Kenneth of the Scots would not have hesitated to use, had he needed to.

It was at Forteviot in 847 that the fate of Pictland was finally sealed. There, Kenneth finished what the Vikings had started eight years earlier. He took advantage of the stability he had secured for Dalriada, whilst at the same time exploiting the disastrous weaknesses of Pictland. In a decisive battle the Scots defeated the Picts and killed the unfortunate Drust MacFerat. With an almost perceptible sigh of relief the line of Pictish Kings came to an end. From this moment on the two lands would be united.

Kenneth did not come to Pictland as a destroyer, although the final crushing of Pictish resistance must have taken some time. For some years to come Dalriada and Pictland would continue to exist as separate peoples. In Kenneth's mind, though, his new realm was a single entity that he quickly came to call Albany. Officially he and his immediate successors were referred to as Kings of Scots and Picts rather than Kings of Albany and this remained the correct style of title until the 18th century. Though a King of England might sit at London in centuries to come, at Edinburgh there would be a King of Scots, and while English monarchs defined their rule in territorial terms, their Scots counterparts defined theirs by the peoples under their protection.

Scotland had been born but it still had a long road to travel to maturity.

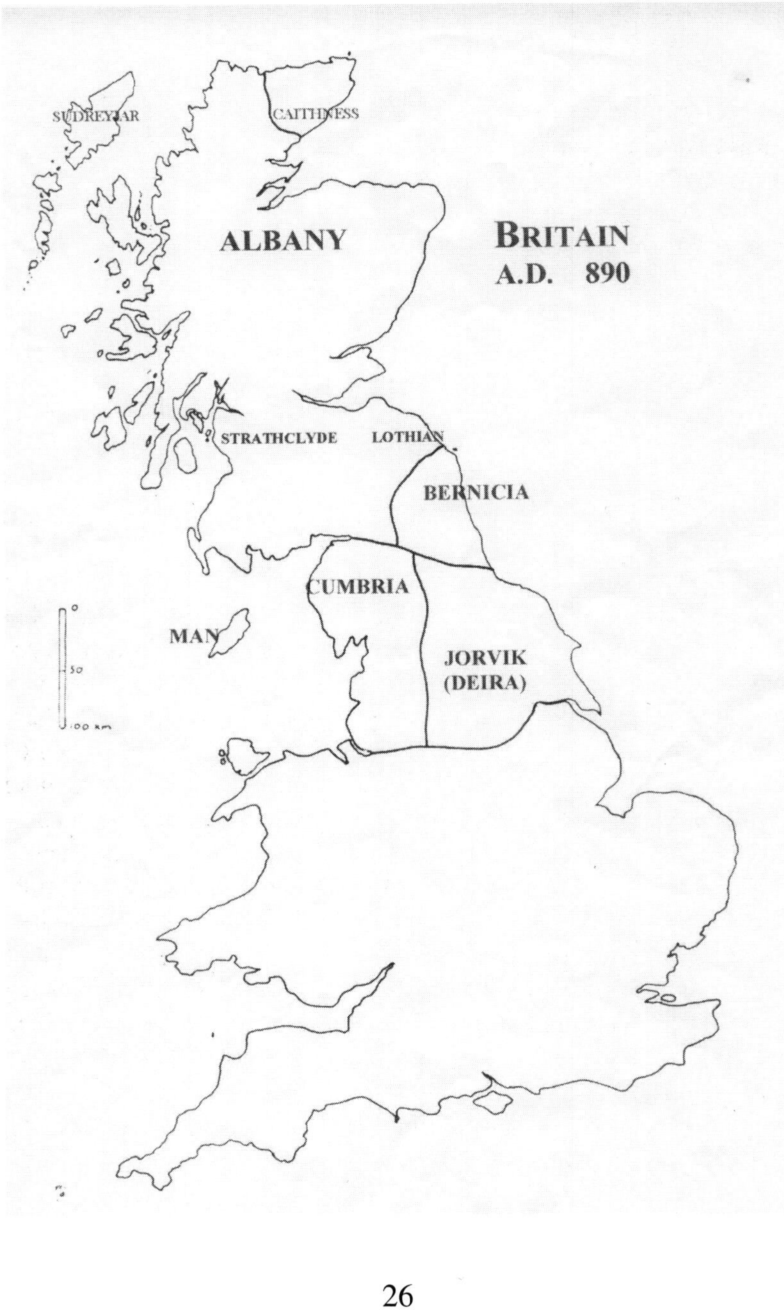
SUDREYJAR
CAITHNESS
ALBANY
BRITAIN
A.D. 890
STRATHCLYDE
LOTHIAN
BERNICIA
CUMBRIA
MAN
JORVIK
(DEIRA)
0
50
100 km

The Viking Encirclement

Before proceeding to the events following Kenneth's death, some comment is necessary regarding the use of place and tribal names. A perusal of history books written during the last two centuries reveals a curious mix. The Picts have also been referred to as the Piks and their name is said to come from the Latin *pictor* (painter) or *picturatus* (painted). All manner of strange tales spring from this name and its alleged Latin root, but the suggestion that they routinely wandered around naked and displaying their painted bodies proves only one thing: that writer has never experienced Scottish weather in the flesh. Whatever the Romans or the Scots or the Northumbrians called them, the Picts called themselves Cruithne. This ancient and long obsolete word has recently been resurrected in the naming of a Near Earth Asteroid, 3753 Cruithne.

The Dalriadan Scots called themselves Scots while the Romans called them Scotti. At least here we have a name that seems to have been more generally used. Its origins, however, are not clear. Legend says that a Celtic Prince eloped with a Pharaoh's daughter, one Scota. Together they fled Egypt, taking with them the rather inconvenient burden of Jacob's Pillow Stone, which became the Stone of Destiny. It has also been suggested, more mundanely, that Scot comes from a word for pirate or sea-raider.

Dalriada itself has a pretty solid history; the major alternative simply involves a slight spelling amendment, Dalriata or Dal riata. The latter is actually probably closer to the original meaning, which is *Riata's holding* from Cairbre Riata. Cairbre was a son of the High King of Ireland who settled first in the north-east of Ireland and then across the North Channel in Alban Dalriada. Legend tells of an argument among his followers, which led to his sea voyage . There may be a grain of truth in the story, as two separate kingdoms, sitting 20 kilometres apart and bearing the same name, is historically very unusual.

As Kenneth began to use the name Albany for his new kingdom he would have been aware that this word had a very ancient pedigree. As Albion it occasionally referred to the entire island that is now called Great Britain. As Alba, Alban, Albania or Albany it had been used for the Kingdom of the Picts which itself has been recorded as Pictland or Pictavia. After union with Dalriada the name came to be used for what is now Scotland north of the Clyde and Forth. Today it is the name the Gaelic population uses for the whole of Scotland.

The purpose of the above diversion is to make a point. Whatever we call historical peoples it is highly likely that they did not call themselves by those names. Equally we can debate as long as we wish as to whether or not the farmers of Kintyre regarded themselves as living within a larger kingdom called Dalriada. Even the Scots, who were perfectly happy with that name, would more likely refer to themselves by their membership of Clans Gabrain, Lorne or Oengusa than by any larger term of identity. We can do worse than note what a 19th century historian wrote when he observed that the terms *Germani* and *Alemanni* were then used quite arbitrarily for peoples who called themselves *Deutsch* and *Schwabe*.

The names we find in history are then simply words used by chroniclers to describe peoples and places. So, in the 10th century, when the term Pict begins to disappear and the term Scot replaces it, nothing horrific has happened to the Picts. The only change is one of terminology.

Terms used from now on will be consistent, even where they might provoke some scholarly nit picking. In dealing with the Roman period, Britannia refers to Roman Britain up to the Antonine Wall. Caledonia refers to all territory north of this and Hibernia to Ireland.

Dealing with the period following Kenneth's union of Pictland and Dalriada, Dalriada refers to the area that is now called Argyll, the regional boundaries are close enough to the ancient frontiers. Pictland refers to ancient Caledonia with the exception of Dalriada. Strathclyde refers to the ancient kingdom of the Britons, from the modern Scottish/English border to the Lennox, north of the Clyde. Lothian refers to the area between the Rivers Tweed and Forth.

Immediately, Strathclyde presents difficulties in that its boundaries extended far to the south of the modern border, becoming confused with Cumbria and the combined British kingdom eventually met with kindred lands in Wales. Such details are certainly worth considering were this a history of Strathclyde or Pictland. Viewed from a Dalriadan perspective, however, we are concerned only with the southward expansion of Albany in a general sense and the effect this had in turning the eyes of the Scottish Kings away from the north and west.

Lothian, too, was the northern district of Northumbria but, apart from temporary raids south of the Tweed, the Kings of Scots had little interest in further expansion down the East Coast. The area did demand constant attention, however. In this we can see a part of the slow but relentless shift in Scots political focus. The great moves south had the inevitable consequence of bringing the Scots into direct contact with their English and, in time, their Danish neighbours.

It is impossible to enter the late 9th century and move into the 10th without reference to the Vikings, and this is the focus of the present chapter. Even here, terminology requires definition. In general, Norwegian raiders visited the islands to the north and west of Scotland while the south-east of what would be England fell prey to Danes. The term Viking will be generally used for these raiders except where clarification is required.

*   *   *

In the year 858 Kenneth MacAlpin, King of Scots and Picts, died. He was probably close to 50-years-old and the illness that killed him was very probably the result of his violent life. As we have noted, Kenneth was a man of his times, but he was no uncultured savage. He certainly subdued remaining Pictish resistance vigorously and ruthlessly. We need no further proof of this than the fact that no Pictish noble ever again laid claim to the throne. After the union of Dalriada and Pictland he also waged war with the Angles and Britons to the south, and by these actions secured his southern frontier. He was clearly comfortable with war, but he also showed a flair for diplomacy.

His formidable strength of character clearly impressed his neighbours, but he also used the ancient expedient of marrying off his daughters to the King of Dublin, to the eventual High King of Ireland and to a Prince of Strathclyde. Within Albany he moved slowly to change established customs, though at the outset made an important concession to the Picts. He moved his capital from Dunadd in Dalriada to Forteviot in Pictland, which had been the Pictish capital. He also transferred relics of St Columba from Iona to Dunkeld, and there established a new spiritual centre for Scots and Picts.

How difficult must it have been to turn away from Dunadd at the heart of the beautiful Crinan Moss? Probably not hard at all, since Kenneth seems to have been something of a gypsy throughout his youth. Dalriada was no more home than Ireland or Pictland; he settled wherever was most suitable.

How trying was it to take the relics from Iona, a beautiful island off the West Coast of Mull in Dalriada? Even easier. Iona was as much a Pictish holy place as a Dalriadan one. Indeed, nearby Mull had long been a place of dispute between Scots and Picts, with the frontier running through it. Any doubts were quickly dispelled by the growing Viking menace.

As shown in the previous chapter, Kenneth had met with Gothfrith MacFergus, King of Oriel in 836. This was the first of many arrangements with either Vikings or descendants of Vikings. Through all of his reign he maintained a very uneasy peace with this rising, turbulent force. In this he had a definite advantage over his fellow kings to the south. Clearly enough of an advantage to move his capital east and leave Dalriada relatively secure, despite its location alongside Viking seaways.

Kenneth was succeeded by his brother, Donald. This may seem unusual, but it was quite common at the time. Indeed the practice of Picts and Scots was to elect the nearest or most appropriate candidate to the throne. This candidate was often traced through his maternal rather than paternal line. The practice has given rise to a commonly repeated error about Pictish succession in particular. It has been suggested that *all* Royal succession was through the maternal line, but this is a misunderstanding.

Some interesting justifications have been put forth for this, including the fact that maternity cannot be doubted, whereas there is always a question about who the father might be. It is inconceivable that a Royal Prince would happily see his claim set aside on the grounds that he might be a bastard on account of his mother's possible infidelities. Equally, suggestions have been made about wives being shared in Pictish society, resulting again in confusion about paternity. This ties in with the previous explanation but it is also suspiciously like the narrative Caesar used when describing British tribal practices in his Gallic War. He stated that these Belgic descended tribes shared women among groups of 10 to 12 men – often of the same family – and any offspring were regarded as the children of the wife's first partner. Caesar was describing what he saw as a primitive and barbaric race indulging in barbaric social practices. True or not, the Britons were, at that time, Pagan. The Picts were Christians, and Christian marriage practice has been largely the same since the time of Christ.

The practice of establishing succession through the maternal line existed to ensure that an adult male was available to take the throne. It is doubtful that the maternal line was regarded as superior to the paternal, but they may have been regarded as equal. So, if the dead king's son was but a child, he would be passed over and the nearest available man would become ruler. Maternal succession was the means whereby the great and unfairly maligned King MacBeth took the throne in 1040.

Clearly this process had the danger that once the king's son achieved majority he might seek the throne in his own name. There are many instances of such princes becoming king after one or more candidates had held the throne before them. Such dangers, though, were infinitely preferable to the calamities that were to befall Scotland centuries later when an endless series of infant monarchs left the kingdom prey to the ambitions of powerful lords and English k+ings. Maternal succession was a sensible and well considered expedient in a time when violence or illness meant that life was short and uncertain. It is unfortunate that it is so often misinterpreted.

Donald ruled from 858-863, and in this short reign continued with Kenneth's efforts to unite the Scots and Picts. He set about imposing Scots Law on the Picts, a move that made him very unpopular. The Picts were never a very united people, but they had many common laws and customs. We have to view Donald with a little sympathy here. Had Kenneth lived longer it would have fallen to him to impose the unpopular new laws. As it was Donald's reign was short and his end uncertain, although it is likely he was murdered.

Kenneth's son, Constantine, followed his uncle Donald and ruled from 863-877. In this succession we see a glaring example of the dubiety of the matrilineal theory; nephew succeeded uncle who had succeeded brother. It should be noted, though, that all of these kings would have been descended from one queen, but also one king (assuming the queen's constancy). Matrilineal succession as an expedient is sensible. As an inflexible policy it is fraught with difficulties.

Constantine's reign is particularly notable for the devastating invasion of Albany by Olaf Gothfrithson, King of the Vikings of Dublin. His was an invasion of a different sort to that suffered by the last Pictish Kings because Olaf stayed. Despite this Constantine remained king and this presents us with an unusual set of circumstances to unravel. Answers may be found in the characters of Olaf and Constantine themselves.

Olaf had made himself King of the Norse Vikings of Dublin in 853. Shortly thereafter he had established alliances with his Danish counterparts, and this combined force raided along the Irish coast and further afield to the Western Isles and the mainland of Albany. In 866 he embarked on the invasion of Albany described above, ostensibly to secure a land route for Viking longships to be drawn across the Forth-Clyde isthmus. Such routes are very common in Western Scotland, and are normally designated by the word *tarbert* or *tarbet*, although most extend from only a few metres to a couple of kilometres wide. Olaf's land route must surely have been the largest tarbert ever utilised, but, then again, Olaf was a new breed of Viking who thought big and permanent. In a practical sense the route Olaf was seeking to secure made a lot of sense. The tidal stretches of the Forth and Clyde are only 60 kilometres apart, compared to nearly 1,000 kilometres around the dangerous north and west coasts.

Olaf's invasion was completely successful. He defeated Constantine but, in a departure from normal Viking behaviour, demanded tribute and then established himself as Overlord of the Scots and Picts – unusual but eminently practical. The Vikings now had unhindered passage throughout Albany, and this situation played a vital part in the subsequent dismantling of Northumbria, to which we will return. Out of the records of this invasion leap two questions: why Overlord and not King, and why did he not simply kill Constantine?

Constantine was the son of Kenneth MacAlpin, and it is hard to believe that, having secured the throne of Albany, he did not have a good measure of his father's shrewdness. The Vikings were a reality that all the kingdoms of the day had to deal with. In the early raiding days their mobility and savagery had, time and again, routed superior standing armies. Now that they were establishing kingdoms of their own they could add strongholds, allies and staging posts to their undiminished fighting prowess. The English kingdoms seem never to have found a way to live with these monsters from across the ocean. The Kings of Albany, though, had managed to secure uneasy alliances and in one way the Viking presence actually worked for Albany.

When Kenneth became King of Scots and Picts his lands, in theory, occupied the entirety of ancient Caledonia as well as offshore islands. Quite how far his claims to the islands extended is anyone's guess, but the reality was that, beyond the islands of

Dalriada, his rule was non-existent. Even among the Dalriadan islands the Vikings were increasingly asserting their control. In the far north of what had been Pictland the King's rule was also in name only. It was in these remote mainland areas and on isolated islands that the Vikings were establishing themselves. If the Kings of Albany could secure a peace with them they could kill two birds with one stone, and the Vikings would inherit the problem of Albany's lawless extremities.

Constantine was also related to Olaf, who had been married to his sister. Subsequently this Overlord of Scots and Picts would marry Constantine's own daughter. The King had been soundly beaten, but within a couple of years he was firmly in league with his Viking master and it was this unholy union that finally brought about the fall of Strathclyde. Olaf, Constantine and Ivarr (King of the Danish Vikings) attacked Dumbarton on the River Clyde to secure the Forth-Clyde tarbert. Dumbarton was the capital of Strathclyde, and with its capture the British kingdom fell irrecoverably under Gaelic rule.

Olaf's Overlordship ended in 871, but we have no clear knowledge of his fate. Constantine carried on as before, though his days as a friend of the Vikings were over. By this time Albany was being regularly used as a through-route for Viking armies moving between York and Dublin; precisely what Olaf had planned, but Constantine had clearly had enough of this ongoing affront to his Kingship.

In 875 Constantine's patience ran out. In that year the King of Jorvik, Halfdan Ragnarson, had set his sights on becoming King of Dublin also. With this in mind he set out to make war in Ireland and, without hesitation, headed through Albany. It must have been with some surprise that he found himself facing Constantine's army attempting to block his path. Whatever he thought of this strange turn of events, his army were seasoned warriors who brushed the Alban forces aside and continued on to Dublin. Once there, with the same effortless disdain, they defeated their Norse opponents and Halfdan took King Eystein's crown.

THE HEARTLAND OF ALBANY

INCLUDING

THE DALRIADAN ISLANDS AND IONA

His triumph was short-lived and the Norsemen of Dublin quickly ejected him. In 877 he raised another army and, clearly regarding Albany as still the natural route between York and Dublin, set out to reclaim 'his'crown. He was untroubled on this march out, but the army he led was tiny by comparison with that of 875 and was soundly beaten once in Ireland. Halfdan was killed in this battle, at Strangford Lough, and his crushed troops made their slow way home. Crushed or not, in Albany they once more met Constantine's army where, again, they won. Constantine was killed in this engagement at Crail, and we have to marvel at the fighting prowess of the Vikings. Worn out by journeying and fighting, returning home from defeat, they still managed to push aside a fresh Alban army on its own soil.

Constantine's brother, Aed, succeeded him as King for only a year until his cousin, Giric, Donald's son, took the throne. The idea of Scotland may have been formed in the time of Kenneth MacAlpin but it was during the astonishing reign of Giric that the nation first took a form that would be recognisable today. The collusion of Constantine with Olaf and Ivarr had brought Strathclyde under the control of Albany but by the time of Giric the relationship between the two kingdoms was far from hostile. It has been suggested that Eochaid, King of Strathclyde, ruled alongside Giric, but the later status of Strathclyde would suggest that he was more likely a junior king, along the long established lines of Scots kingship. In modern terminology we are familiar with the ranks of, for example, earl-duke-king or lord-prince-king. The Scots usage was similar, but it was clear that all of the parties were regarded as kings. The *Ri* was the King of a small kingdom. The *Ruiri* was the Great King of a larger confederacy and the *Ri Ruirech* was the King of Overkings. It may seem like simple semantics, but there is a profound difference between a prince in the modern sense and a Ri in the ancient. King Giric and King Eochaid appear to have been very close and, as Eochaid was very young, Giric effectively adopted him as his son.

Eochaid was the son of Rhun, and his proper name was Eochaid Map Rhun. This is clearly not a Gaelic name, and demonstrates that, even at this late date, Strathclyde was still a nation of Brythonic (British) rather than Goidelic (Gaelic) Celts who looked south into Cumbria and beyond to Wales for their heritage. For all the closeness of Giric and Eochaid this difference was to have a sad conclusion.

Both Kings ruled from 878 until 889, and in this time made the most spectacular advances. Together they freed Albany from the grip of the Vikings, and separately pushed their respective lands south – Eochaid into Cumbria and Giric into Lothian. At the same time the once great kingdom of Northumbria was finally dismantled and re-built by the Vikings and the Angles, occasionally working together.

Northumbria in 866 comprised three main areas. In the south was Deira. To the north of this was Bernicia and, further north, Lothian. Lothian had been constantly harassed by Kenneth MacAlpin, who saw the southward expansion of Albany as inevitable and essential to the long-term security of his realm. Giric finally fulfilled Kenneth's ambition in 878 when he pushed the Angles south of the Tweed.

Though it would take some years to realise, Lothian was destined to be a twin edged sword. Its acquisition, along with that of Strathclyde, meant that for a very brief time the whole of what is now Scotland became a Celtic nation with a distinctly Gaelic culture. It has rightly been described as the only nation of any significance in the divided Celtic world. The world of the Brythonic Celts never found stability again after the passing of Strathclyde and Cumbria. In time, the last vestiges of this culture, in Wales and Cornwall, would fall under English domination, where they defiantly remain to this day.

The term *twin edged sword* generally implies that there was good and bad in the described situation. However, we are dealing here with history and there is no telling what outcomes might have arisen had different decisions been made. Lothian gave the Scots a resolution to their long battles with Northumbria and then Bernicia. A border was finally established along the River Tweed, where it remains to this day. It also allowed the Scots to consolidate the nation's defences in the face of the developing English nation to the south. England might have been late arriving, but its constituent parts were, even then, a vast and immensely populated place when compared to Scotland.

Lothian also exposed Scotland to English influence. It had been the northern part of the Anglian kingdom of Northumbria for centuries, and it was the place to which Saxon refugees fled from troubles in the south. As the attention of the Kings of Scots turned away from their traditional heartland north of the Forth and Clyde, so slowly did the Gaelic culture begin to decline. The fact that Scotland is today an English-speaking nation has to be recognised in part for the common error, particularly among the English, that, at some point, it was subdued and taken over. No such event ever took place, but to this day there is a common misconception that Great Britain and England are one and the same place, with Scotland occupying some nebulous identity as a conquered state vaguely tagged on. Scotland remains a separate nation within Great Britain, and it speaks English because it naturally, over centuries, adopted the language of its larger, more powerful and politically more influential neighbour to the south.

Which edge of the sword covers the above? Ultimately it depends nowadays on whether you believe in Great Britain or not. Many Scots do not and an increasing number of English are calling for their own nation to be more clearly defined, without the complexities and vagaries of just what modern *Britishness* means. Good or bad, Lothian brought Scots and English culture into close contact.

The other edge of the sword was unquestionably bad, although it would be more than a century before this would become apparent. In 1031 the King of England, Cnut, visited Malcolm II, King of Scots. This is a considerable jump in time from the period now being explored but what happened during that visit was a direct result of the Scots annexation of Lothian and it would prove to be a disaster for Scots independence right up to the final union of the two nations nearly seven centuries later.

There is some dispute as to whether Cnut visited or invaded Scotland. An invasion was quite within his powers but he would have faced the same difficulty that all subsequent English invaders would meet. To move beyond Lothian and into what had been Pictland any invader has to cross the River Forth at Stirling Bridge. A properly coordinated defence can inflict horrific destruction on an attacker here, as Edward I was to discover when his army encountered the forces of Sir William Wallace almost three centuries later. It seems likely that Cnut moved through Lothian and met with Malcolm before any further move north was necessary.

The importance of Stirling Bridge cannot be overstated. Historically it was the only viable route north. To the east was the long Firth of Forth and to the west vast tracts of marshland right up to the Highlands. It was also such a psychological barrier that early maps show Caledonia as a virtual island, with the Forth and Clyde meeting at Stirling Bridge. Clearly this is a huge exaggeration but any large army had to come this way. Any other route was simply unworkable.

The Anglo Saxon Chronicle records that Cnut received the submission of three Kings at this meeting. These were Malcolm II himself, MacBeth (then a sub-King of Moray) and Margad, the King of Dublin. The submission was specifically restricted to Lothian and certain small territories adjoining it. At no time did Malcolm submit to Scotland becoming a sub-kingdom of England, but this was to be the lie that would be thrown at the Scots for the next half millennium. At the time Malcolm would have barely given the matter any detailed thought. He paid the required tribute for Lothian and Cnut left in peace. There was no way to know that Wallace's defence at Stirling Bridge three centuries later would be one direct result of this carelessly given oath which, ironically, Malcolm had no intention of honouring in the long term. He was not a great keeper of oaths.

But these events were to happen in the future. In 878 King Giric secured Lothian and rightly regarded the acquisition as a success.

In 867 the Vikings had taken York, and from then on Deira was ruled directly by them, although it would be some years before the Kingdom of Jorvik was formally created in place of the older Anglian territory. In Bernicia, the Vikings placed a puppet king but, it is noteworthy that this land was never overrun by either Scots or Vikings. Indeed relations between Jorvik and Bernicia became so normalised that, for a time, after 877, a Bernician King, Egbert II, ruled Jorvik during a period when, after the death of King Halfdan in Ireland, the Vikings were without a King of their own. It seems that politics is a timeless science, although another almost unthinkable suggestion has been made – that the Vikings wanted to settle and raise families and were not in the least averse to Anglian rule.

In 889 Giric and Eochaid were deposed by Donald II, the son of Constantine. Whatever the relations between the Vikings of Jorvik and their Bernician neighbours, Donald was faced with a unique situation. This king, who was the first to be called Ri Alban (King of Scotland), was surrounded by Vikings. To the south of Lothian was Bernicia, which was allied with Danish Jorvik. To the south of Strathclyde, Cumbria was coming under growing influence from the Norse Vikings of Dublin, who also ruled Man. To the west and north the islands were no longer Albany's, indeed Orkney was now sufficiently powerful that its earl was turning his attentions to the Alban mainland.

Donald almost immediately began losing territory to the Vikings but it was the same territory that had worked to Constantine's advantage. Donald had little hope of effectively ruling the far northern areas of Caithness and Sutherland and their acquisition by the Earl of Orkney allowed Albany to focus on the south, particularly Strathclyde. This southern focus would dominate Albany's political and military policy from now on.

Donald's kingdom was very soon called Scotland and the name Albany became an historical usage. This Scotland embarked on integrating Strathclyde fully into the realm and, in the process, extinguished the ancient British heritage of that land. Donald sent the British nobility into exile, and it is likely that Eochaid and

Giric joined the exodus south to Wales, where there was a kindred culture. As well as the many sent away, many more must have left of their own accord. The Gaelic culture being imposed upon them would simply have been too alien. Perhaps this was for the best but the loss of an ancient culture is always a sad event.

Covering this period in the history of Great Britain many works focus their attentions to the south and the developing Saxon kingdoms. There is merit in this, given the enormous import that the future kingdom of England would have, but it does Scotland a great disservice not to recognise this one point. That Scotland was a unified nation, occupying roughly its modern boundaries, at a time when England was ruled by seven independent kings.

MacBeth

There are two MacBeths; the villain of Shakespeare's wonderful play, and the strong and wise king who actually ruled Scotland from 1040-1057. This chapter will deal with the latter, although some explanation will be given as to why Shakespeare felt it necessary to malign him so viciously and unfairly.

It may seem strange to divert to a character such as MacBeth in a work dealing with Dalriada and Argyll, but this man had a closer link with the ancient Scots Kingdom than is commonly realised. He was also the last genuinely Gaelic ruler of Scotland, and deserves some attention for this. Soon after MacBeth's death Malcolm Canmore would set the trend for all future Kings of Scots by turning his back on Scotland's Gaelic and Pictish past. From Malcolm's time onwards Scotland would look southwards and take its lead from the Anglo-Norman world that was developing there.

MacBeth MacFinlay was born around the year 1005, the son of Finlay, Mormaor of Moray and Ross, the most influential noble of his time. His mother was Donada, a daughter of King Malcolm II. Even by Gaelic usage his Christian name is a little unusual in that it looks like a surname; it means *Son of Life*. As a grandson of King Malcolm, MacBeth was of the royal line, but it was initially unlikely that he would succeed to the throne as his descent was through a female line. Here we have to return to the issue of matrilineal succession, and can see that in this case the female line was certainly not regarded as superior to the male. MacBeth was, in 1040, *elected* to the throne, though mainly due to the fact that the dead King Duncan's sons were both children. This may have been the last instance where the ancient, and eminently sensible, Scots practice of choosing the nearest adult male was used.

MacBeth's father, Finlay, was the Mormaor of Moray, which was one of the original sub-kingdoms of the Picts. The title

Mormaor equates roughly to that of a modern Earl, but these rulers rightly regarded themselves as junior kings along the ancient Scots and Pictish usage. Where these Mormaors fit into our picture is that they were descended from the Dalriadan Clan Lorne. As was described in the first chapter, this clan was effectively neutralised as an independent power in 736 at Loch Linnhe. However, the demolition of a royal house's power does not necessarily mean that its aspirations are in any way diminished. In the 21st century the Royal House of Stuart still exists, in exile in France, where Prince Michael awaits the call from the Scots to return home.

Nurturing a belief that they had an equal claim to the Kingship of Dalriada, but harder pressed by Viking raids than their stronger kin, the clan migrated out of Dalriada and north-east into Pictland. When Kenneth MacAlpin established Albany, Clan Lorne joined with the northern Picts in their long resistance to the new kingdom. In time, and after much assimilation with the Picts, all reference to Clan Lorne was abandoned and the chronicles generally speak of 'the men of Moray'. This kingdom was to remain practically independent of Scotland until the opening years of the 13th century.

Moray resistance to Scotland eventually evolved into a less warlike, but still hostile, independence. In some ways this was not dissimilar to the position taken by the Western Isles and Caithness, but in those remote places there was no question of the Scottish crown disputing their independence. Moray was different. It was too large and far too close to the heart of the kingdom to be allowed any genuine autonomy. By the time of Malcolm II – MacBeth's grandfather – official Scottish policy was to subjugate this region.

Around 990 Finlay became Mormaor of Moray and, as usual, ruled the area with little regard for his supposed King. The extent of his disdain for Scotland is demonstrated by his taking battle north and into Caithness against Earl Sigurd of Orkney in 995. The significance of this act is that Finlay plainly saw his position as identical to Sigurd's. This was a major error of judgement. Scotland might be compelled, at times and by circumstance, to overlook some of the attitudes of these northern Mormaors, but they were still subjects of the crown.

When Malcolm II became King of Scots his approach to Moray was decisive, if not immediately comprehensible. In 1008 he married his daughter to Earl Sigurd of Orkney. This act seems, at face value, to be simply a means of securing the good will and support of Caithness against the challenge of Moray's independence. In fact, Malcolm's intentions ran much deeper.

Despite having lost against Earl Sigurd, Finlay still managed to extend the power of Moray right across the north of Albany. The effect of this was that north of the Great Glen, Albany exercised no real power. In truth this had always been the case, but the Earldom of Orkney had tended to be a less turbulent influence here than Moray. By the marriage to his daughter, Malcolm bound Sigurd to himself as family. He now had Moray pressed between Albany and Caithness, but he was not satisfied to leave things on this secure, if warlike footing.

As was common practice when bringing another noble into the Royal family, Malcolm granted Sigurd certain territories. Unfortunately these were between Caithness and the Great Glen – lands that Finlay regarded as being within his sphere of influence. At the same time, though, he also granted Sigurd lands within Moray itself. In one perfectly legal move the King of Scots had firmly put the upstart Mormaor in his place.

In granting to Sigurd lands to the south of Caithness and into Moray, Malcolm had also handled two political difficulties with the deftness of a chess player. On the one hand he had boldly stated that Moray was subject to the Scottish crown, and on the other he had established himself as Sigurd's Overlord. Had he insisted on being Sigurd's King this would have brought him into conflict with the King of Norway, whose subject Sigurd was legally.

The above might seem like legalistic nit-picking, but by these actions Malcolm was making a subtle statement: The Earls of Orkney might rule Caithness in the name of the Norwegian King, but the addition of lands in Sutherland and Moray, granted by the Scottish King, created a larger territory over which the King of Scots would now have some degree of authority. Once again, after Donald's almost successful consolidation of Scotland around the year 900, the Kingdom had roughly the borders we know today.

Parts of Moray might have had an Earl of Orkney as their ultimate Lord but its rulers continued in their resistance to the Scottish Crown until MacBeth became Mormaor in 1031. Aged 27, he was considerably less hostile than his predecessors who had continued with the age-old pretensions of Clan Lorne, and had actively sought to depose King Malcolm. If proof is needed of Moray's change of policy, it was noted before that MacBeth was one of the Kings who submitted to King Cnut, along with King Malcolm, over the subject of Lothian.

A remarkable point about this meeting with Cnut relates straight back to Dalriada. When Malcolm died three years after the meeting, he did so without a male heir. This made him the last male descendant of Kenneth MacAlpin. The royal line of Clan Gabrain was dead. MacBeth would live for a further 23 years and, although he could not know it in 1034, he would have no sons either. When he died, the pretended royal line of Clan Lorne would die with him. Of course this comment ignores the use of matrilineal succession, but in reality the die was cast. The Dalriadan line was dead, and the Gaelic culture that had grown from it and flourished would soon begin a long, slow decline that is sadly continuing to this day.

MacBeth became King of Scots in 1040, having succeeded his cousin, Duncan, who had, himself, succeeded Malcolm II in 1034. As stated before, MacBeth, during his rule in Moray, was in no way hostile to the Scottish crown, as his predecessors had been, but he still had a strong sense of Moray's independence. When Earl Thorfinn of Orkney decisively routed King Duncan during a disastrous Scottish campaign in the north, he made the mistake of retreating into Moray.

Moray had for years been no friend of the Vikings, but it was not prepared to join with Duncan under any circumstances.

Not being hostile to Scotland was far from being the same thing as supporting Scotland. MacBeth allied himself with Thorfinn in an effort to eject the remains of the Scots army from Moray territory. In this he was totally successful. Duncan's final military outing, at the end of a shockingly mis-managed and ill-conceived series of campaigns in Caithness and Northumbria, ended in his death at Pitgaveny in August 1040.

Duncan's calamitous military adventures did not, unfortunately, represent the full extent of his foolishness. Whilst he certainly burned with his grandfather's ambition, he had none of his powers of leadership. He was also incapable of exploiting useful weaknesses in England and Caithness. During periods of instability in these lands he did nothing. And he was unprepared for an attack from Bernicia in 1038, which seems to have been retaliation against the now dead Malcolm for an assault decades earlier.

When Duncan finally acted it was in 1040, when he felt he was ready, and with little regard for the external realities of the time. His attempt to wage war against both England and Caithness at the same time was bound to fail. It has been a well worn and utterly reliable guide for commanders from ancient times to the present day, that a war on two fronts can seldom be won, and should only be embarked upon under two sets of circumstances. One of these is where victory is beyond any degree of doubt, and the other is where you have absolutely no other choice.

Little has been recorded of Duncan's non-military exploits but it says enough that he was not mourned. He was ambitious but lacked talent, and he was ruthless but lacked focus. It is one of the great mysteries of Scots history, exactly why Malcolm II sponsored this disagreeable lout when he had at least one other suitable candidate in MacBeth. Malcolm had no sons, so succession passed through his daughters to their sons. As Duncan's mother was older than MacBeth's there was a tendency to err towards her son, but when MacBeth married Gruoch he acquired a stronger claim through her, as she was the granddaughter of Kenneth III. Such were the complex lines of claim, running through male and female lines, but always likely to be over-ruled by the great lords of the realm if there was a need.

Duncan left an heir but, as he was only a child, the Scottish Council quickly elected MacBeth as King. We will deal with Shakespeare's version of his life later but a very brief history will suffice to demonstrate that he was a good, strong and wise king. He established a close relationship with Earl Thorfinn, who was also his half-brother. Time and again we have seen that blood is definitely not thicker than water in dynastic matters, but the two appear to have been genuinely close, and this defused the long running animosity between the Scots (including Moray) and the Norse.

In 1050 MacBeth went to Rome where he is recorded as having distributed money generously to the poor. Such pilgrimages were the aim of all Catholics at the time, and it is strange to consider that at this time the Church was undivided in the west. It should be pointed out, though, that a king could only make the long trip to Rome if he was leaving behind him a secure and stable kingdom. This visit demonstrates another face to MacBeth. He was much more than just a military leader; indeed he was one of the few early Kings of Scots who perceived his role as anything other than a military protector and levier of taxes. He was also a devoutly religious man.

The extreme shortness of the above comments is the best testimony to MacBeth's rule. Apart from a brief rebellion by his uncle in 1045, MacBeth's reign is marked by peace, progress and prosperity. Indeed, when this secure world began to unravel, the source of its undoing came, not from within Scotland, but from England. From all that we can gather, MacBeth was a much loved and respected King within his own realm.

In 1054, Duncan's son Malcolm was 23, and not at all disposed to accept the idea of a king, elected by the Scottish Council, usurping his rightful claim. This was another example of possibly the only weakness in the Scots idea of nearest adult male inheriting. At some point those dispossessed children became men and sought what they regarded as their rightful inheritance.

Malcolm had been brought up at the English Court from childhood, and this influence was to change the course of Scottish history and identity to the present day. When he presented his claim he was fully supported by Edward the Confessor, although there can be little doubt that this King of the English could see great benefits in supporting a compliant Scottish puppet.

Edward made a substantial force available to Malcolm, commanded by Earl Siward of Northumbria, and this army moved into Scotland. At Dunsinnan, in July 1054, MacBeth engaged the enemy and was convincingly beaten. The Scots managed to inflict enough harm on the invaders, though, to force both armies to withdraw from one another. Malcolm retreated into Strathclyde, and from this base engaged in three years of increasingly successful civil war. With each reverse, MacBeth was pushed further and further north until he reached his Moray homeland but, even there, his retreat continued.

Comment has been made about the racial make-up of the two armies and it is an interesting fact that large numbers of Viking descendants faced one another in the many engagements. Indeed it has been suggested that there was a noticeable Dane/Norse split on the English/Scots sides. This was undoubtedly true but it is perhaps a fact that speaks more for the racial melting pot that Britain always has been – Norse, Dane, Pict, Celt, Briton, Gael, Saxon, Angle, Norman; but all distributed about the island and taking up arms under banners other than their original ethnicity.

At Lumphanan, near Aberdeen, in 1057 MacBeth and his bodyguard were ambushed and cut down. His stepson, Lulach, was elected to succeed him but this gesture was only delaying the inevitable succession of Malcolm III, The Bighead (*Canmore*). In 1058 Bighead was crowned at Scone Abbey. It was the beginning of the long, slow end of the Gaelic culture, and the definitive end of Dalriada.

So how did a strong and noble king become debased into the deceitful monster of Shakespeare's play? How did the 27-year-old military incompetent, Duncan, become elevated into the

'Venerable Duncan' of the same play? MacBeth's wife was the gentle and much loved Queen Gruoch, who became, under Shakespeare's skilful pen, the vile Lady MacBeth. And just where did the non-existent Banquo fit into the whole marvellous, slanderous genius of it all?

The above questions can be answered in one name, which we will come across again in this history: King James VI of Scots and I of England. Aware of the poor image of the Scots in London, not least his own, he practically dictated the details of Shakespeare's tragedy, lifting his details from distorted histories by Boece and Hollinshed.

Remotely descended from Duncan, James had MacBeth become the villain of the piece. Keen to link the Stewarts to the ancient Celtic Kings, Banquo (MacBeth's fictional friend and fellow General) was taken from Boece. The Stewarts had originally been the Stewards of the Royal House, whose nobility had ultimately been elevated to the position they had once served. And James seems to have taken a nasty swipe at his detested wife, Anne, by creating the unforgettably inhuman Lady MacBeth, again with creative input from Boece. The many character assassinations can perhaps be understood but Queen Gruoch's implication in Duncan's murder when he was killed in open battle is perhaps a slur too many. Shakespeare's MacBeth, for all its magnificence, is just an early example of a blatant fiction masquerading as historical fact.

MacBeth's stepson, Lulach, was elected King after his death, but Malcolm Canmore continued to press his own claim to the throne. Lulach's seven months on the throne were marked by continuous war, and he was killed at Strathbogie in 1058. King Malcolm III was crowned at Scone Abbey on April 25, 1058 and ruled until 1093. An entire history could be written about this coarse ruffian, who slowly changed into a civilised ruler and devoted husband, but his importance to this work is that his rule marks a very clear ending of Gaelic dominance in Scotland.

Malcolm III was the 58th king since Fergus the Great founded Dalriada in 498. It is extremely telling, therefore, that so many lists of Scottish kings begin with him. In this Malcolm would be proud, for his view of history was strictly forward. He had little time for backward looking sentimentality (as he saw it), and he boldly set about changing Scotland. Whether his subjects agreed with him or not proved to be irrelevant, as the momentum he engineered was unstoppable.

Were it not for Malcolm III, it is doubtful this work would be written in English. Had MacBeth been permitted to live out his reign in peace, it is quite possible that Scotland would be, even today, a Gaelic speaking country. But such are the twists and turns and possibilities of history that it might just as easily have ended up being written in Norse.

If the Gaelic world was fated to fade and be assimilated into the English-speaking world, then it is perhaps fitting that its last King was MacBeth. This fine, strong, devout and compassionate man lies buried on Iona, where he was despatched from this world with all the honours due to a revered King.

The Lords of the Isles

'Without Clan Donald there was no strength. Without Clan Donald there was no joy'. (Clan MacDonald website)

The mighty Clan MacDonald once ruled lands that occupied large parts of ancient Dalriada as well as islands beyond the ancient frontiers. While the extent of their territories did not match Dalriada exactly, there was a close enough correlation to confirm that this land was (and is) quite distinct from the rest of Scotland. The mountains and ocean define the area quite clearly and naturally, and it is hardly surprising that the modern governmental area of Argyll is practically coterminous with Dalriada.

Clan MacDonald can be traced directly back to the 12th century warrior Somerled, who restored the Gaelic culture in the Western Isles, and resurrected the Dalriadan claim to Kintyre, Lorne and Argyle. As his distinctly *unScots* name suggests, Somerled was of mixed Viking and Scots blood. His father was Gillebride, Thane of Argyle, who was descended from King Ragnall of York, a Dane. To further confuse his bloodline, his mother was Norse, the daughter of Earl Sigurd II of Orkney. It was she, in Ireland in 1105, who gave her newborn son his name that means *Summer Voyager*.

Somerled's early years are vague, but by 1130 he was Thane of Argyll and a loyal subject of the King of Scots. Indeed before 1140 he had been entrusted with command of King David's West Highland forces. About the same time he married the daughter of King Olaf of Man, and by this union cemented his attachment to the Gaelic and Viking cultures of the West Highlands and Islands. Such a position set him at odds with the Scots Kingdom but, in these early years, Somerled believed that he might persuade the King to turn back to Scotland's Gaelic roots. This might seem naïve, looking at events with the benefit of hindsight, but the rapid anglicising of Scotland was less than a century old at this time. In the north and west the new Anglo-Norman culture was making little headway, indeed it was faced with a vibrant and thriving melting pot of Viking and Gaelic cultures. The long years of cultural suppression were still centuries in the future.

In 1153 Malcolm IV became King of Scots and Somerled appears to have attempted to turn the young monarch's mind towards his Viking and Gaelic subjects. Finally realising that the time for persuasion had probably passed long before he was born, Somerled rebelled against the Scottish crown. This rebellion involved no direct assault on Scotland, but Somerled let it be known, by his actions as much as by his words, that his realm was now fully divorced from that of Malcolm.

In 1154 Olaf of Man died and his son, Godred, became King. After the usual round of initial purges and slayings, though, Godred did not settle down to rule his islands. Instead he became increasingly despotic, ultimately taking on all of the attributes of a tyrant. As has been lamentably repeated too often down through history, Godred did not have the sense to know when to stop. There comes a point when even the most loyal of subjects will rebel, when he realises that nothing, even total subservience, will please his lord. Godred's nobles reached this point quite quickly, and an offer was made to Somerled whereby his son, Dugall, would be made King of the Isles, in the place of Godred. Somerled's side of this deal was to crush Godred's power.

For a Gaelic lord to even think of engaging the Vikings in battle was remarkable, even if that lord was as much Viking as Gael himself. For that lord to imagine that he could defeat the Vikings on the open seas was patent lunacy. Yet this was exactly what Somerled had in mind. There can be little doubt that Somerled was familiar with Viking ship technology. Argyll is a maritime region, which looks out to the Inner Hebrides on the west and to Arran and Bute on the east. Sea power was the key to supremacy in this area.

Dalriada was always a Kingdom dominated by the sea and from its earliest days the waters of the North Channel and the

Sound of Jura were busy with vessels of all sizes. These were, for the most part, built for purposes of fishing and transport. The advent of the Viking longship quickly handed domination of the seas away from the Scots to the new arrivals. By the time of Somerled this was still the case but he had, for years, been experimenting with the traditional methods of shipbuilding and had come up with a remarkable new design.

The Viking longship remained the champion of the seas in the 12th century. The boats were never as long as the monsters often portrayed in Hollywood movies, but could still carry a formidable contingent of fighting men. They were also extremely manoeuvrable and very fast. It was these attributes that Somerled had to match and, if possible, defeat. To begin with, he concentrated on the longship's weaknesses.

Viking vessels of this period were steered by a steerboard, which was mounted at the rear on the right hand side. It is from this device that the term starboard (for the right of a ship) comes. The steerboard was operated from a tiller that reached across the stern of the vessel. This system was efficient in the hands of a skilled steersman, but Somerled discovered that a hinged rudder, mounted on the centreline of a boat at its tail was more efficient, making it much easier to handle.

The longships were also very frail considering the fighting purpose for which they had been designed. This is always the way with any functional fighting system: speed can be acquired at the expense of strength or vice versa. Anything that tries to achieve the best of both worlds will end up deficient in all areas. The Vikings had opted for speed and stealth, reasoning that once at the heart of the battle their own fighting prowess would carry the day. Somerled realised this and installed sniper positions at the top of his vessels' masts. From these lofty vantage points his troops could bring down fire from above onto the open and defenceless longship decks.

In January 1156 King Godred of Man took his fleet north to crush the pretender to his throne and his upstart father. Off the coast of Islay the fleets engaged in a battle that carried on through the night. Anyone who has witnessed the dark grey waters of the Atlantic in winter can imagine the biting cold through the 16 hours of darkness that prevail at that time of year. When the sun finally rose, Godred's fleet was ruined and Somerled was the victor.

Somerled's victory was remarkable. At this time Godred's fleet was the most powerful in Britain or Ireland. He should have won, but Somerled's innovations defeated the Vikings at every turn. Every well-tried and efficiently executed tactic was soundly beaten. By sunrise the King of Man had nothing left to throw at the forces of this Thane of Argyll, but even in defeat he still had diplomacy for Somerled's victorious fleet had been savagely mauled by the Vikings. So badly, in fact, that it was utterly incapable of delivering the coup de grace. Godred was defeated but he was not destroyed.

Negotiations followed and Somerled secured possession of the Hebrides south of Ardnamurchan, including Kintyre. Godred retained Man and the Hebrides north of Ardnamurchan, and by this he presumably hoped to contain Somerled, for his temperament remained brutally despotic. Realising that no sustainable peace could be pursued with such a volatile neighbour, Somerled prepared his fleet in 1158 for a second engagement.

The ships that had so successfully defeated Godred's longships in 1156 were called Nyvaigs (*small ships*) and it is from this name that the stronghold of Dunyveg acquired its name, Dun Nyvaig (*the Fortress of the Small Ships*). It was here, at Lagavulin Bay, on the south coast of Islay, that Somerled's fleet was based. In 1158, 53 of these small ships descended on Man and put Godred to flight.

Even as King Godred fled to Norway, Somerled's troops devastated Man. It would be pleasing, as a Scotsman, to report that the massacres and pillage that followed were in some way provoked but this was simply the brutality of an unrestrained conqueror. Even religious sanctuaries were violated as the Gaels secured the island.

Somerled now ruled Islay, Jura, Mull, Coll, Tiree, Scarba, Colonsay, Gigha, Kintyre, Knapdale, Lorne and Argyle, as well as the smaller islands in this area. He assumed the title Rex Insularum (*King of the Isles*), and this was accepted by the King of Norway. Two years later King Malcolm reluctantly accepted the title also. Malcolm's delay in accepting the reality of Somerled's rule seems perplexing. He had no authority over the islands, including Kintyre, so why would he be in the least interested in this change of ruler?

Had Somerled been lord of only the isles it is possible that Malcolm would have shown little interest in him. The Overlordship of the King of Norway in the islands was a fact accepted by all in Britain at the time. The King of Scots had nothing to gain by crossing his Norwegian counterpart other than the acquisition of a territory he could never hope to control. Unfortunately Somerled was the Thane of Argyle, and this position, which translates as Earl or Ruler, was subject to the Scots crown, in theory at least.

From 1153, when King Malcolm succeeded King David, and Somerled was actively promoting the interests of the Gaelic/Viking west, the young King was also being pressed strongly by his advisers. These were all strongly influenced by the Anglo-Norman culture of England; indeed many of them were Norman nobles. As such they had the same ruthless political ambitions of their southern cousins and could see no benefit to the Scottish crown in tolerating a lawless territory on its western frontier. Piece by piece the King was persuaded that Argyle had to be brought, unambiguously and indisputably, within the Kingdom of Scotland.

From 1160, though, King Malcolm officially accepted Somerled as a brother King of the Isles. The issue of the mainland territories remained unresolved but such a vague diplomatic issue was not going to remain unaddressed forever. For the time being, however, Malcolm and Somerled were on the best of terms; even when it came to war there seems to have been little personal animosity between them. Somerled acquired a nickname at this time; *Sit-by-the-King* suggesting that he had a genuine fondness for his young Scots counterpart, and was in close and regular contact with him.

In 1164 the honeymoon came to an end, when Somerled raised an army of 10,000 men in the hope of compelling Malcolm to come to terms over Argyle. It is initially unclear whether Somerled himself initiated this campaign or if it was a reaction to moves by Malcolm. Later actions of the King of Scots prove that Somerled was, in fact, getting his retaliation in first and had cleverly anticipated an attack on his own lands.

Somerled's force was despatched in a great fleet of 160 vessels that sailed up the Clyde to Greenock. From this landing point his army advanced east to Renfrew, where the Scots army was waiting. Even at this late stage, with his lands effectively invaded, Malcolm hesitated to engage in battle. There is evidence that his fondness for Somerled was undiminished but Malcolm relied heavily on his councillors and these were now seeking to convince the King that Somerled's true intention was to invade Strathclyde and Lothian. Malcolm plainly saw through this ruse, seeing that the issue at stake was still the status of Argyle. Instead of accepting the need to attack he sent the Steward of Scotland, Walter Fitzalan, to negotiate terms.

Malcolm re-stated his position regarding the Kingdom of the Isles. He had no designs on these territories, which he regarded as Somerled's by right, his wife being the daughter of the Earl of Orkney. There was absolutely no doubt, also, that the King of Norway was the feudal superior there. On the matter of Argyle, Lorne and Kintyre, though, he demanded their immediate 'restoration' to the Kingdom of Scotland.

The inclusion of Kintyre in Malcolm's demand is strange as it was always included among the Isles. Magnus Barelegs had, at the end of the 11th century, claimed all of the Western Isles, including Kintyre, as possessions of the Norwegian Crown. Kintyre had acquired its definition as an island by a rather insolent, pedantic interpretation of the treaty terms that had been granted by Malcolm Canmore. The Norwegian King was to possess all islands to the west of Scotland. The only restriction on this was that King Magnus had to be able to round the claimed island in a ship, 'with the rudder or steerboard properly set'. Magnus was no fool and could see that Kintyre was a rich and fertile territory, probably bettered only by Man. Seating himself on the after-deck of a small skiff, Magnus had his vessel dragged down the Tarbert Isthmus from east to west, rolling on a trackway of logs. King Malcolm Canmore was, at this time, preoccupied with hostile actions against England and gave the loss of Kintyre little thought. In truth, it is doubtful he would have cared in any case. As has been recorded before, his interests lay in the south.

Somerled had received the demand of the King of Scots, and his response embodied the essential belief of all subsequent Lords of the Isles. He re-stated his right to the Isles, which seems superfluous since Malcolm had happily supported him in this. There was, however, a point to this. Somerled reminded Malcolm that his predecessors had come into possession of the Isles by an edict of King Eugenius the First. Appealing to ancient right was a common thing and Somerled was taking his claim right back to the roots of Scotland.

Eugenius, if he ever existed, lived in the late 4th century, and is recorded as having been killed by Magnus Maximus, then a general in the army of Theodosius the Roman Emperor. Maximus definitely fought in Britain at this time, during a period of civil unrest. Although given the dignity of a King at a later date, Eugenius was more probably the leader of an army of Irish mercenaries defending Irish territories against the native Pictish armies.

Having stated the basis of his claim to the Isles he then reminded King Malcolm that the Vikings had dispossessed his forefathers. The Kings of Scots had offered no assistance at that time, and the Isles were at the present date held by Somerled as a subject of the Norwegian King. In short, his claim to the Isles was ancient and even now, as a subject King, he owed no allegiance to the King of Scots.

Turning from the Isles, he then addressed the matter of the disputed mainland territories with devastating bluntness. He had as a good a right to Argyll and Lorne as he did to the Isles, and he had proven his right to the Isles. He then professed his friendship for King Malcolm and offered his assistance in any other matter. But, as long as he breathed, he would not surrender any of the rights that he currently possessed.

Having received Somerled's reply, Malcolm still hesitated. He had no personal dislike of Somerled, and the two men appear to have been on friendly terms in the years prior to 1164. But he had to do something and he had no desire to see war waged on his lands.

In 1160 Fergus of Galloway had rebelled against what he saw as King Malcolm openly subordinating himself to King Henry II of England. This charge was understandable but it was actually quite unfair. The specific offence that had so incensed many Scots was Malcolm accompanying King Henry to Aquitaine in 1159 to wage war against the Count of Toulouse. In fact, Malcolm was not fighting as a subject King. He actually owed King Henry certain feudal duties for lands that he held in England.

Before becoming King of England, Henry had promised King David (Malcolm's grandfather) that he would surrender Northumberland and Cumbria to Scotland when he ascended the throne. This promise was quickly forgotten but, in 1157, Henry made Malcolm Earl of Huntingdon in consolation for the undelivered territories. It was this grant of land that put Malcolm under feudal obligation, *but only as Earl of Huntingdon.* This holding of lands in both Scotland and England by Scots nobles would eventually lead to the confused loyalties that so typified the wars of independence that finally led to Bannockburn.

Malcolm was young, but when the need was upon him he could act decisively. Calling on his Anglo-Norman nobles he crushed Fergus in a series of expeditions. Four years later he was faced with a similar problem with Somerled, much as this King of the Isles was protesting his friendship for the King of Scots. It has been suggested that Malcolm's councillors carried out the events that followed, with little knowledge on the part of the King. Unfortunately, his decisiveness in putting down Fergus' revolt suggests that he was more in control than he let history subsequently believe.

Having despatched his reply to King Malcolm, King Somerled waited. He did not have to wait long. The morning after sending his reply he was found murdered in his tent along with his son, Gilliecolum. His killers were never identified, although legend has it that Malcolm's councillors somehow persuaded Somerled's own nephew, one Maurice MacNeil, to do the deed. It is said that he was so stricken with remorse that he also stabbed one of Malcolm's men who had roughly handled Somerled's corpse. Malcolm is then said to have pardoned the youth, which, if true, implies that he was a little closer to the murder than he would have liked thought. The truth is we will never know who killed him, but Somerled was gone.

The discovery of their leader dead spread confusion among the Islesmen, who swiftly decamped and returned to the fleet at Greenock. Bizarrely, they left their King's corpse where it lay, although it has to be conceded that they were far from home, in an essentially foreign land that spoke a different language and facing an enemy army. Perhaps they were right. This was no time for grand funereal gestures.

Whether or not King Malcolm was directly involved in the murder he did right by his dead rival. He had Somerled's corpse carried to Iona where he was buried in a manner appropriate for a Dalriadan ruler. Malcolm had, after all, never disputed Somerled's right to the Kingship of the Isles. And, on Iona, Somerled still lies. There is no support for the later suggestion that he was reinterred at Saddell Abbey in Kintyre.

After his death, Godred II returned and regained the Northern Hebrides and Man. The rest of Somerled's kingdom was divided between his sons. His eldest son, Dugall, who had been set up as a future King of the Isles by Godred's nobles, in fact became Lord of Lorne and Argyle (along with Mull, Coll,Tiree and Jura). His second son, Ragnald, took Islay and Kintyre while a third son, Angus, became lord of Arran and Bute.

From 1164, the three brothers ruled their various parts of the kingdom with mixed degrees of friendship and co-operation until 1192, when Ragnald and Angus fell out. The reason for their dispute is not clear, but after 1192 Angus is recorded as the undisputed ruler of Arran. This suggests that either Ragnald was the actual ruler of the island prior to this date or some sharing of power existed. At the same time Dugall's possessions passed to Ragnall and we may assume that Dugall had died at this time. This may have been the source of the friction between Angus and Ragnall, as the younger brother saw more and more territory passing to his older brother while his own possessions remained small and disputed.

From 1192 Ragnall began to style himself King of the Isles and Lord of Argyle and Kintyre. In effect, he ruled what had once been Dalriada. It should be pointed out that all three brothers had the right to call themselves King, which they did when it seemed appropriate, but, prior to 1192, they did not habitually use the title. Although there was no issue of one brother holding seniority over the others it was the line of Ragnald that became the primary line of the Kings of the Isles.

King Ragnald, like his father, had a deep respect for the better aspects of both the Viking and Gaelic cultures of the west. He was also a devout Christian who founded monasteries and rebuilt war-damaged churches. He brought the Cistercian Order to Saddell Abbey in the early years of the 13th century and it is this act which may explain the unfounded story that he reinterred Somerled at this same abbey. He also established an Augustinian nunnery on Iona.

Ragnald's older brother Dugall is not so well recorded by history. In spite of his right to the title King he seems to have followed a policy of loyalty to King William of Scots (The Lyon). He was the ancestor of Clan MacDougall, and, while not a direct progenitor of Clan MacDonald, both his son and grandson would, in time, become Kings of the Isles.

In 1210 Ragnald died and his son Donald became King. The Kingdom he inherited, though, was not the new Dalriada of his father. His cousins, Duncan and Dugald, sons of the late Dugall, took possession of their father's former territories, which had been held by Ragnald until his death. This effectively restricted Donald to Kintyre and Islay, but from this heartland of the kingdom, his fleet controlled the coast of Scotland.

This Donald was the ancestor of Clan MacDonald but anyone looking for nobility, at least in his early years, would be sorely disappointed. All the subtlety of his father and grandfather were lost on Donald who was essentially a Viking raider at heart. In some respects, though, this was fortunate, for his cousins, Duncan and Dugald, were of similar temperament and spent the next two decades terrorising the Isles, including Man.

The date of Donald's death is not known. It may have been anytime between 1249 and 1269 and has even been suggested as prior to 1230, although this leaves a disturbingly large interregnum to explain. What is more certain is that it was the activities of his maurauding cousins that occupied the energies of the other rulers of the time. It is clear that Donald changed his ways as he became older and sought absolution for his countless sins by making a pilgrimage to Rome. His cousins, Duncan and Dugald, showed no such improvement in their characters and by 1230 their activities became too much for King Haakon of Norway.

Haakon's aim was to put Duncan and Dugald's younger brother Gillespie (known also by a Norwegian name, Uspak) onto the throne. In this he failed, but only because Uspak was killed. The other part of his plan was achieved though, and Duncan and Dugald were forbidden to use the title King, which was bestowed instead on King Olaf of Man. This unhappy man spent his entire life attempting to secure his rights as a subject King of the Norwegian Crown. When he died, he was preparing to travel to Norway to receive a dressing down for surrendering naval service to the English Crown, which had conveniently forgotten that Man and the Isles were not English possessions.

For 18 years the Kingship ceased to have the clear definition that Somerled had acquired for it. Duncan and Dugald continued to rule, but only as lords and subjects of the King of Man. Eventually Haakon relented and the Kingship was restored to Ewen MacDougall, son of Duncan and Great-Grandson of Somerled. In 1249 King Harald of Man, still senior to Ewen, was drowned at sea and Ewen was named as his successor. For a brief moment it looked as if the Kingship of the Isles would be vested in the descendants of Clan MacDougall, but trouble was brewing in Scotland and Man.

In Scotland King Alexander II was preparing to wage war against the west. Only his timely death saved the Isles but in the south Ewen's Manx subjects were not prepared to accept him as King. In 1252 he went to Haakon in an attempt to have his Kingship confirmed but the Norwegian King was of no mind to foist an unpopular ruler on his own subjects. Ewen was deposed by his Overlord and King Magnus was set up in his place. Ewen remained for a time in Norway as a naval officer, but in 1255 he went to Scotland where the young King Alexander III treated him well. From this point on he regarded himself as a Scot and never swerved from his loyalty to the Scots crown.

When Ewen changed his allegiance his cousin Dugald, a grandson of Ragnald, was proclaimed King of the Isles by his followers. King Haakon confirmed this assumption of authority, and from then on Dugald was as unmoving in his allegiance to Norway as Ewen was to Scotland. This was to have tragic, if not fatal, consequences for Dugald after the events of 1263, when Haakon sent an expedition to enforce his rights to the Western Isles.

In October 1263, after gathering his fleet at Gigha, Haakon sailed into the Firth of Clyde to teach the Scots a long overdue lesson. Unfortunately King Alexander III was ready for this ill-advised adventure. After the Norse defeat at Largs Dugald continued to fight against the Scots Kingdom. Even when it became apparent that Haakon's successor was prepared to negotiate terms for a transfer of the Isles to Scotland Dugald continued to fight and he remained a renegade Viking warrior until his death in 1268. The final tragedy of Dugald's life is that as he attacked Scots ports and shipping he plainly regarded himself as a legitimate warrior fighting for his sovereign. Unfortunately that sovereign had irrevocably surrendered his 'Southern Isles', which would never again fall within the Norwegian sphere of influence.

Haakon's successor, Magnus, finally agreed the Treaty of Perth in 1266, which passed the Hebrides to Scotland. Both the Scots and the Norwegians have claimed the Battle of Largs as a victory for nearly eight centuries but regardless of which side was in better shape at the end of the day, the Norse had failed in their attempt to compel the Scots to recognise their sovereignty over the Isles. Magnus took a long, objective view of the situation and finally recognised that the Isles were becoming ever closer to Scotland and ever more remote from Norway. He took the sensible route and rid himself of possessions that could only become thorns in Norway's side in the long run.

A fact often neglected about this Norse expedition was that its failure did not immediately result in the loss of the Isles by Norway. Haakon and then Magnus remained firmly in military control for the moment. In 1264 King Alexander sent a force to take the Hebrides and Man, and it was during this engagement that a son of Donald, grandson of Somerled, became prominent. This was Angus and it was through him that Clan MacDonald achieved its supremacy amongst all other lines of Somerled's descent, even more senior lines.

Although it is not clear exactly when Angus came into his title, by 1260 he was ruling Donald's lands as Lord of Islay. In this capacity he was a subject of King Haakon but he seems never to have regarded his duties particularly seriously. When Haakon sent his fleet against Scotland in 1263, Angus had to be compelled to fulfil his obligations. The Norse achieved his support by taking his son hostage. A year later he was obliged to submit to the King of Scots and again his loyalty was enforced by his son being taken by the Scots. Despite this the Scots also compelled Angus to sign a declaration stating that he would be dispossessed of all of his possessions if he again changed sides.

Many Islesmen must have shared the torments suffered by Angus at this time. Loyalty was not taken as lightly in the 13th century as it is today, and this pressure to support first Haakon and then Alexander must have been extremely distressing. It is a measure of how seriously this issue was regarded that Angus' son was made a hostage twice. In the case of King Alexander, it is plain that he regarded Angus' support for Haakon as disloyalty to Scotland, hence the demand that he undertake in writing not to switch sides again. Alexander clearly saw Angus as his own subject, even while he held the title to Islay from Haakon. All of this confusion, though, would be settled when the Isles passed to Scotland in 1266.

With the issue of sovereignty now resolved, Alexander set aside any doubts he might have had and appointed Angus King of the Isles. There is no doubt that King Angus now made the necessary oaths and became a subject of King Alexander. It is a mark of the trust that Alexander now had in Angus that he interfered very little in the future running of the Isles.

Angus ruled until 1296, and he secured the support of other island nobles very quickly. Even the more senior descendants of Somerled soon recognised his seniority, and by the time of his death he was known as Angus Mor (the Great). His MacDonald descendants would be Kings and then Lords of the Isles for the next two centuries.

It was Angus' younger son, also called Angus, who secured for the MacDonalds the base of power that would eventually lead to their dominance in the Highlands and Islands. It was this Angus Og (The Young) who supported Robert Bruce while he was on the run from the English in 1306. In the fullness of time this support led to King Robert confirming Angus as King of the Isles and bestowing on him a senior honour to that held by Clan MacDougall who had supported Bruce's rival, Balliol.

Angus' son, John, became Lord of the Isles in 1330 and, despite a very uncertain loyalty to King David of Scots, he managed to extend MacDonald power to the Outer Hebrides and then to the remaining northern isles. By 1340 he controlled all of the Hebrides. His son, Donald, attempted to extend the power of the MacDonalds into the heartland of Scotland in 1411. In this he was unsuccessful, but his failure was far from devastating militarily. Its real failing was that it created a sense, among the Scots, that these Islesmen were a savage and primitive tribe whose culture was quite distinct from their own. The irony here could not be less subtle, that these descendants of the Dalriadic Scots finally found themselves regarded by a mongrel nation of Picts, Scots, Saxons, Normans and others as not being true Scots. Indeed the term 'the wild Irish' has been used of these Hebridean clansmen. Of course the Islesmen were not pure blood Scotsmen either, but there is still a bitter sense of prejudices to come in the mainland's view of them at this time.

In 1423 Donald's son, Alexander, inherited the Isles from his father, and Ross from his mother. This made him the most powerful Lord in the Highlands and Islands but he came into his inheritance at a time when King James of Scots was determined to impose his will on the north. The King was ultimately successful, but only after years of conflict with Alexander and other Highland lords. Alexander was eventually subdued but his son, John, carried on his father's implacable hostility to the Scottish Crown. Indeed he went as far, in 1450, as to declare his territories independent of Scotland.

For a Highland lord to believe his lands quite separate from Scotland was hardly new. Argyll was described often as being separated from Scotland by the Drumalban Mountains, so clearly the notion of Scotland, as it existed in the minds of its Kings and ardent supporters, often differed from the day to day reality of the inhabitants of its wilder extremities. This said, the lengths John was willing to go to secure his independence seem quite extreme.

In 1462 John and the Earl of Douglas signed the Treaty of Westminster-Ardtornish. By this treaty, (which acquired its title from a palace of King Edward IV of England and a castle of John of the Isles), the earl of Douglas and John MacDonald of the Isles became subjects of the King of England. This astonishing act meant that, if Edward conquered Scotland, then John and Douglas would share what had once been Pictland, north of the Forth. In fact, fired by Edward's support, John became, for a time, effectively King of Scotland in the Highlands and Islands.

The chaotic state of Scotland had to be resolved and it was realised by the councillors of the nine-year-old King James III that the only way to negate the Treaty of Westminster-Ardtornish was to come to terms with England themselves. This took until 1464 at which time John was compelled to renew his allegiance to the young King of Scots. By 1473, however, he was again taking up arms against the Scots Crown.

By 1475 John had been declared a traitor. His lands were forfeited to the Crown and an army had been despatched to arrest him. John was saved, however, by the intervention of the Earl of Argyle who pressed for his re-instatement. This was agreed, but from now on the lordship of the Isles would be held as a Scottish peerage and not as an independent earldom along the ancient lines. The Scottish Crown did, however, clip John's wings to some extent. He was denied the earldom of Ross.

John's son, Angus, objected to the new order, which would deny him an independent lordship after his father. In 1480, in direct defiance of John and the King, Angus raised an army and set out across the mainland in a rampage of destruction. The pretext for the invasion was an alleged insult against his sister, Lady Margaret, by her husband, Kenneth of Kintail, a MacKenzie. Whether or not Kenneth actually insulted the noble lady is open to dispute, but Angus' response was, to put it mildly, excessive.

Angus' army included islanders as well as MacDonalds from Lochaber, Glengarry and Knoydart. This force marched up the Great Glen, following the route taken by Clan Lorne centuries before, and seized Inverness, where Angus declared himself King of the Isles. He then moved north to the fortress at Dingwall, which he took, fortified and held for the next two years.

In 1482 an army was finally raised from MacKenzies and other clans who hated the MacDonalds. Under the Earl of Atholl, they were crushed at Lagabraad, compelling the Crown to build another, which had greater success. Angus was forced to withdraw into Lochaber. Even in retreat, Angus inflicted sufficient damage on his pursuers that eventually only his father, John, remained in the hunt. An attempt to reconcile Angus and John failed and at the end the conflict was to be MacDonald against MacDonald.

Most of Clan MacDonald took the side of Angus Og, but John rallied the support of Clans MacLean, MacLeod and MacNeill. These two forces met, at sea, near Tobermory in the battle of Bloody Bay. This was an engagement that the Vikings would have been proud of and at the end of the slaughter, John was utterly defeated. Angus, already self-declared King of the Isles, now announced that he was the head of Clan MacDonald. Unable to dispute the issue any further, John retired from actively pursuing his claims and Angus set about ruling his kingdom.

Despairing of defeating Angus in open battle his enemies now removed his son, Donald Dubh (the Black), from Islay and placed him in the 'protection' of the three-year-old boy's grandfather (ironically the Campbell Earl of Argyle). Angus Og responded in typical fashion when he launched a ferocious assault against the lands of the Earl of Atholl, who had plotted young Donald's kidnap. Atholl and his Countess were taken prisoner, but Angus released them after a year, convinced that he was the victim of supernatural retaliations for violating the sanctuary they had been hiding in.

The young Donald Dubh seems to have been an important figurehead because this poor soul was to spend most of his life in prison. In 1488 Angus, while taking an army against Inverness again, was murdered by an Irish harper, The Lordship then returned to John but he appears, on account of his age, to have deferred to his nephew, Alexander of Lochalsh who acted on behalf of Donald Dubh. Regardless of this professed 'regency' in Donald's name, or perhaps because of it, Alexander was determined to take Ross and through 1491 and 1492 he led an army through the area, again capturing the much abused Inverness, until he was injured and captured.

James IV, King of Scots, eventually had enough, and in May 1493 he formally forfeited the lands of John II, who was still officially the Lord of the Isles. The Lordship was finished but the MacDonalds were still a formidable force. Unfortunately they were faced, in James, with one of the most able kings that the Stewart dynasty ever produced

King James was a rarity in that he took the time to visit his possessions in the west. He moved persistently and showed leniency wherever he thought it would not be abused. In general all lords were instated in their existing lands but now as subjects of the Scottish Crown rather than the defunct Lordship. Of course, some nobles lost lands, but few were as flagrantly opposed to the new situation as Sir John of Islay who had lost lands in Kintyre. In 1494 he stormed Dunaverty Castle and hanged the Royal Governor in the sight of the King himself. It goes without saying that Sir John did not live long after this outrage.

In 1498 John II died. The Lordship of the Isles was no more but there was still a descendant of the line of Somerled who might prove to be a thorn in the side of James' new policy in the west. Donald Dubh was still a prisoner at the castle of his grandfather but, in 1501, he was liberated by his kinsmen and taken under the protection of his uncle, Lord Torquil Macleod of Lewis.

Whatever Donald had been taught as he grew up at the home of the Earl of Argyle it did not lead to him becoming a loyal subject of the Scots Crown. In 1503 he, and his protectors, led another rebellion through the Highlands. King James reacted swiftly, but it took until 1505 to capture Donald who was imprisoned at Edinburgh Castle. It is difficult to justify rebellion against a legitimate ruler, particularly one as able as James IV, who even went as far as to learn the alien tongue of his Island subjects, but it is harder to justify the fact that Donald Dubh was held a prisoner for a further 38 years. The mystery attaching to his incarceration is quite why James just did not have him executed for treason.

Donald escaped from Edinburgh Castle in 1543 and immediately rallied the support of the island lords. This tenacity and the ease with which he could summon the support of the MacDonalds perhaps explains why the Scots King found it so hard to deal with this most irksome of subjects. In 1545 Donald held a great Council of the Isles, and there declared his allegiance to the English Crown. In this act we finally see clearly just how distinct the Islands felt themselves to be from Scotland.

To this day, the thought of a Scotsman swearing allegiance to the authority of England remains an absurdity. The Scots have been among the most patriotic of Britons, but Bannockburn left a memory that will not permit them to easily transfer their loyalty to their southern neighbour. Clearly, the islanders felt no such revulsion to such a step and were prepared to align themselves with whatever power would guarantee their independence. They had, after all, been subjects of Norway before becoming subjects of Scotland and both kingdoms had essentially left them to their own devices. A Kingdom of the Western Isles, subject to England, would have presented no absurdity to them, so any suggestion that Donald was in some way a traitor to Scots ideals carries no weight whatsoever.

As things turned out Donald's plans never achieved fruition. On the way to pay his allegiance to King Henry VIII of England he became ill and died in Ireland at Drogheda. The Lordship of the Isles had been gone for some time, but with the death of Donald Dubh, grey haired and with only the memories of decades of imprisonment, the very idea died too. From now on the west would be a part of Scotland, legally at least for the sense of independence and difference would continue. No ruler, even after the passing of the Lordship, could be absolutely certain of the support of Argyle and the Islands.

At first glance the policy of breaking the Lordship seems sensible but what King James did not realise fully was that this system of government had actually served the Isles well. Feuding and bloody conflict occurred, but in general most Clans had deferred to the Lordship, and this had maintained an imperfect degree of peace. Perhaps the MacDonalds could have maintained their pre-eminent position among the island clans, even after the passing of the Lordship, but, unfortunately, government policy increasingly erred towards breaking MacDonald influence as well as its power.

The end result of the government's strategy was that the feud became an increasingly vicious aspect of clan life. As the MacDonalds were slowly dispossessed of their powers, others that had never held any ascendancy began to rise. Having tasted a little power they then began to seek more and, in a strictly organised world of territories and seniorities, one clan could only improve itself at the expense of another. For the Highlands and Islands the passing of the Lordship was a calamity, but it would be some time before the full ramifications would become apparent.

On top of the problems of clans striving to better themselves was the matter of the Scots government being seated firmly in the Lowlands. At this time the language of the Lowlands was Scots but it doesn't take a degree in linguistics to see that Scots is a dialect of Old English. In every way, from culture to language, religion to history, the Highlands and the Lowlands were different worlds. They were also far apart, physically and emotionally.

Distance prompted the Scottish government to implement a policing procedure that was to have brutal results in coming centuries. Rather than attempt to control the savages of the Highlands and Islands directly from Edinburgh, the task was delegated to certain loyal clans. As the clan situation degenerated in what had once been Dalriada, the Crown now added a new trouble.

Clan Campbell was to be one of the houses that would maintain the King's peace in the west. This clan would slowly advance itself, often at the expense of the MacDonalds, but it would also find itself, at times, pursuing aims that were quite at odds with those of the Crown. It would also find itself severely maligned for the methods it used in pursuing its own improvement, although fairness demands that we recognise that every clan looked to its own before any other. Most, though, never achieved the heights secured by the Campbells.

A final note deserves to be added to this chapter. It has been noted earlier that the Scots of the Lowlands had begun to regard the Scots of ancient Dalriada as little better than savages. It was around this era that these selfsame descendants of Dalriada begin to reject the title 'Scots', presumably because of the derisive way they were perceived by their Lowland countrymen. That ancient name of Albany was again resurrected, now as Alba, and the original Scots began to name themselves Albannach, a name that continues to this day among the Gaelic speaking population.

Earlier chapters have indicated that such matters are generally simply matters of semantics. The term 'Britons' is today used for all citizens of Great Britain, and extends to the Province of Ulster as well, which is not within Great Britain. It is simply a term, and it is doubtful that any modern Briton pays much attention to the fact that the word was once used for a very specific group of ancient British tribes. The replacement of Scot with Albannach was different though. This was a last attempt by an ancient race to assert its difference from a more powerful neighbour, which had essentially stolen its identity.

The decline of Clan MacDonald set in motion a general decline of the Gaelic culture that was probably only completed in the 20th century. In islands such as Gigha, there were still people being born in the early 20th century who could speak no English. Such a situation no longer exists, and Gaelic is now a language spoken only by those with a specific interest in either it, or the culture that spawned it. Whether this is a tragedy or not depends on your beliefs but it can be confidently stated that without Somerled and the Lords of the Isles, it is very likely that the Gaelic culture would have died centuries ago.

Gaelic is hardly thriving in these early years of the 21st century, but it is still there. I suspect that it will continue for as long as the culture that spoke it is remembered and revered. Which is no more, really, than it deserves.

Clan Campbell

'The House of Argyll, as the head of the Clan Campbell, holds such a prominent place in our national history, its records are so intimately blended with every struggle for religious and political freedom, the actions of its chiefs have shed such lustre on our annals, that any fresh fact connected with their history cannot fail to be acceptable to the public'.

The above was written in the preface to a long out of print history of *The House of Argyll,* written in 1871. Two unusual things immediately leap out of these fine and admiring words. The first is that the sentiments expressed are most emphatically not shared by a great number of Scotsmen. The second is that they are true, for this clan has had more than its share of glory. Unfortunately no other clan has ever been so completely identified with its shameful moments, and these have come to overshadow a remarkable history.

During the reign of Malcom Canmore, in the 11th century, Archibald Cambell (the usual spelling, outside of the clan itself, until the 16th century) married Eva, the daughter of Paul O'Duihne. Paul was the lord of the lands of Argyle, or Lochow as they were then known. He was a descendant of an ancient Fingalian hero, Diarmid O'Duihne, the mighty boar hunter of Kintyre and it is from this source that the Campbells received the boar crest that remains a part of their heraldic badge. In an echo of matrilinear succession, the family continued to be known as Clan Duihne (or sometimes Clan Diarmid, Duihne's son) in Gaelic and Irish genealogies, although the clan did adopt the surname Campbell after Archibald's marriage to Eva.

This strange mix of ancient clan identity and modern (post-Canmore) use of a surname is actually not just a matter of tradition. In 1370 King David II granted a charter to Sir Archibald Campbell. This referred to the lands of Craignish, and ratified Sir

Archibald's right to these *'...in as ample manner as his ancestor Duncan MacDwine held his barony of Lochow'*.

As to the origins of Archibald Campbell himself, this is less sure but the likeliest answer is that he was a Norman noble who arrived with William the Conqueror in 1066, although he may have been a British noble from Strathclyde. We can be certain, though, that he came from a distinguished background as Clan Duihne were, even then, an ancient family and undoubtedly choosy about who their daughters married. It has also been suggested, less convincingly, that Archibald came from a subject clan and, in a practice found in other clans, presented a fictitious lineage to validate his assuming a lordship to which he had no natural claim.

As to the origins of Clan Duihne, we have already mentioned the great boar hunter, but his line is said to have descended from the legendary King Arthur and, by a long and winding route, via the French royal house, it reached Ireland and then Alban Dalriada. It has also been suggested that the clan's ultimate roots lie in ancient Egypt, although this is likely simply an extrapolation of the legend of Scota.

As well as being a mighty hunter, Diarmid O'Duihne was also a renowned warrior who is reputed to have come to Scotland in the 10th century to check the growing Viking menace. Having succeeded in this role he settled in Argyle and married. The act that made the boar the symbol of his family occurred at Glen Shea in the Grampians, where he killed a boar so large and aggressive that it had killed several hunters already. Whilst he succeeded he was fatally injured in the process and died shortly thereafter.

Diarmid's elder son was Arthur Armderg (Red Armour). This name came either from the colour of his war kit or from the fact that it was routinely drenched in blood. It was through Arthur that the family line continued but Diarmid is also said to have had a son, Malcolm, who went to Normandy and married the heiress of Beauchamp, a niece of William the Conqueror. The significance of this Malcolm is that an alternative form of Beauchamp was Campusbellus, clearly creating a lineage for Archibald decades later. We should disregard this information but it has to be said that most of the information surrounding Diarmid and his descendants is mythical. This has to be distinguished from being fictional, though. There is clearly a considerable body of truth in the stories but it has all become heavily mixed with legend.

Arthur's eldest son was Paul MacDuihne who was later called Paul-a-Sporran as he was the treasurer to King Duncan and later to Malcom Canmore. He excelled in this important role and was created a knight, Sir Paul of Lochow. When Sir Paul died his brother, Arthur Cruachan, became protector of his niece, Eva. It is at this point that the origins of Archibald Campbell become important.

Determined that Sir Paul's possessions should not fall into the hands of another clan, Eva resolved only to marry one of her own kin. So when Archibald, second son of Malcolm MacDuihne, visited the family, a match was made and these cousins were married. Archibald brought the name of his mother's possessions to the union, Campusbellus in Normandy. He also brought a symbol that he had adopted from the family of Beauchamp, the *gyronee of eight*, a shield cut in eight pieces, which represented the shield having been repeatedly slashed in battle. This symbol still forms a part of the arms of Clan Campbell and also the modern governmental territory of Argyll and Bute.

The corruption of the name Beauchamp into Campbell provokes immediate suspicion but, interestingly, it has been suggested that Archibald's younger brother, Dwine, fought bravely on the Norman side in the conquest of England, and became the founder of the Beauchamp Earls of Warwick. The Earls of Warwick are reputed to have always been on the friendliest of terms with the Earls of Argyle, addressing one another as brothers. Another suggestion has been made that Dwine, who was also called Gwine, was the famous Guy, Earl of Warwick. Again, it is easy to dismiss such tales, but there is a legend that one Guy, son of the Earl of Warwick's Steward, fell in love with the Earl's daughter. To prove his valour one of his tasks was to kill a boar – a Campbell symbol.

In truth we will never be able to pick apart the strands of fact from legend. The name Guy appears many times in relation to the Earls of Warwick. In one tale, one Guy kills a mighty African giant, and it is this story which comes closest to the great Celtic warrior tradition, where immense courage was never regarded as a bar to a hefty dose of exaggeration.

Returning to Archibald and Eva, they had a son, Duncan MacDuihne Campbell who married Dervail, the heiress of Cruachan. Thus, in two generations, and through female lines, the lands of Argyle were united under the Campbells. Duncan died around 1097 and was succeeded by his son Cailein Maol Maith (Bald Good Colin), the 3rd Campbell. He married a niece of King Alexander, and was the first Campbell to distinguish himself by his extreme devotion to the King of Scots

In 1110, he and his troops were all killed at Dunstaffnage Castle, protecting King Alexander from rebels. Cailein was Justice General, Master of the King's Household and Lord of the Isles at the time of his death. These powerful positions and the undoubted loyalty of the Campbells were to be the founding stones from which the clan's future prestige would grow. It has been observed that although the Campbells never sought to wear the Royal Crown, they carried it for the King. They were also instrumental in the setting up and bringing down of Royal houses.

Cailein was succeeded by his son, Sir Archibald Campbell, who was followed by Sir Duncan, whose son was another Archibald (often known as Gillespic). Archibald married Errick, daughter of the Lord of Carrick, and by her he had a son, Cailein. It is with this descendant, Cailein (Colin), that the Campbells move out of the realms of myth and tradition and into well-recorded fact.

For all the scarcity of information about the Campbells in the generations immediately before the birth of Cailein, it is fair to assume that they continued in their energetic loyalty to the Scots Crown. We need only record that Cailein was one of the great men summoned to Berwick in 1291, as part of Robert Bruce's party, in the dispute over the Scottish succession. Only the head of a powerful and respected clan could hold such an eminent position.

As is well recorded King Edward, having been asked to adjudicate on the matter of the Scottish succession, selected John Balliol rather than Bruce. This choice created no automatic difficulty for Sir Cailein. At this time the Campbells were very much a minor power in the West Highlands. The MacDonalds were the Lords of the Isles and, through their kin, the MacDougalls, also Lords of Lorne. None of these clans paid very much attention to either the King or the rest of the Scots kingdom, and they pursued their own interests quite unmindful of any external issues.

The Campbells had, for some time prior to the succession crisis, been involved in a dispute with their neighbours, the MacDougalls of Lorne. As with all clan issues this had simmered away for years, with no sign of an imminent solution. It is not certain what the original argument had been about, as is often the way with such matters. When the Campbells had taken the side of Bruce, the MacDougalls had sided with Balliol, but this did not escalate the issue. It was only to be expected that opposing clans might take opposing sides in a national dispute.

Two things occurred in 1294, which pushed the tense standoff between the Campbells and MacDougalls into open war. John Balliol was now the de facto King of Scots, but his rule was a degrading experience for him, as he had been compelled to accept King Edward of England as his Overlord. Despite this, he set about ruling his kingdom and rewarding those who had supported his claim to the throne. One of these was the MacDougall Chief, Alexander of Lorne, whom John made King's Lieutenant. This clear display of favouritism infuriated Sir Cailein but it was the second occurrence that finally brought the clans to blows.

The Campbell possessions then extended from the northern part of Loch Awe northwards to the great Ben Cruachan. Unfortunately, the southern marches of these lands had no Cruachan to clearly mark the line between Campbell and MacDougall territory. In fact, finding any sort of natural boundary within this wild and difficult terrain is impossible. The disputed area appears to have been around Loch Tralaig in the String of Lorne, and in 1294 a ferocious battle took place there.

Sir Cailein led his troops and from the start the Campbells had the upper hand. The MacDougalls fought bravely, but the action was a constant slow retreat for them until, finally, their line collapsed and a chaotic retreat rapidly became a terrified rout. Seeing his enemy fleeing east, Sir Cailein allowed his enthusiasm to get the better of his normally reliable good sense, and he fearlessly pursued them as far as Loch na Sreinge, about three kilometres east of Loch Tralaig, and two kilometres north of Loch Avich. There, the MacDougalls put up a desperate defence during which Sir Cailein was hit by an arrow and killed instantly.

The death of the Campbell commander put fresh heart into the MacDougalls and they now swept forward to soundly defeat the enemy that had so recently seemed on the verge of a brutal and decisive victory. In the aftermath Sir Cailein's body was recovered and taken north to Kilchrenan, close to Loch Awe, where he was interred and remains buried to this day.

The death of Sir Cailein coincided with the final years of the rule of Angus Mor, the MacDonald King of the Isles, when MacDonald power began its remarkable ascent. This rise, coupled with the convincing defeat at Loch na Sreinge, effectively neutralised any further expansion of Campbell power for a long time to come.

To this day Sir Cailein is remembered in the Gaelic surname of the Duke of Argyll, Mac Cailein Mor (Son of the Great Colin). His son, Sir Neil Mac Cailein Mor-na-Sreinge, succeeded Sir Cailein. This rather complex surname is a memorial to the place of his father's death. Sir Neil was clan chief during the turbulent years after the junior Robert Bruce had proclaimed himself King of Scots in 1306.

During his famous flight to the West Highlands and beyond to the Islands, Robert Bruce was supported and protected by Sir Neil Campbell. Strangely, considering the way their paths would diverge in the future, the MacDonalds of the Isles were also strong supporters of King Robert. In 1307, King Edward, The Hammer of the Scots, died while marching north against the Scots. His son, Edward II was probably not the spineless weakling legend has created but he was never the soldier that his father had been. Despite having been charged by his dying father with continuing the war in the north, Edward II stood the army down and returned home.

The respite that Edward's death gave him allowed King Robert to secure his position within Scotland. In 1309 he moved against the MacDougalls of Lorne. This clan had vigorously opposed Robert's claim to the Scots throne. At the Battle of Methven, three years before, they had been a part of the largely English force that routed Robert's army. One of the MacDougalls is reputed to have torn a brooch from the breast of King Robert at this battle, and to have then held to it firmly despite Robert crushing the man's skull with his war-hammer. This brooch was said to have remained in the possession of the MacDougalls for many centuries.

Sir Neil Campbell, who also provided the necessary equipment and men for the adventure, reconnoitred the King's route to Kintyre and safety in 1306. All along that perilous trek the MacDougalls were the clan to avoid. They may have been related to the MacDonalds, but in the matter of King Robert's claim to the Scots throne they doggedly followed their own path of opposition.

In the end their opposition cost them dear. It would be easy to lay the charge of treachery at the feet of the MacDougalls, but it simply does not stick. This was a time of political turmoil when there was no way to avoid taking sides. The MacDougalls chose their side and stuck with it to the very bitter end. Near Ben Cruachan in 1309 the King's army crushed them. Bruce's men garrisoned their stronghold at Dunstaffnage, and the great days of the MacDougalls passed away.

Sir Neil was steadfast in his support for Robert Bruce, and after Bannockburn was well rewarded for his many brave and selfless services. Again, it would be too easy to see self interest in his support but it only takes a moment's consideration to see that it was by no means certain that Bruce's party would succeed. The dangers and the privations Sir Neil suffered along with his King were very real and he must have been constantly aware of the revolting death suffered by Sir William Wallace. There were three courses open to him: victory, defeat or betrayal. The third course never once tempted him.

In 1308, Sir Neil, backed by Sir Gilbert Hay and Sir Alexander Seaton put their seals to a solemn declaration *'to defend with their lives and fortunes the liberties of their country, and the rights of Robert Bruce, their King, against all mortals, French, English or Scots'*. This declaration was made at the Abbey of Cambuskenneth and is ample proof of this knight's dedication as the threats to his position were very close in those early years.

In 1314 he was one of the barons at the Parliament at Ayr who legally recognised Robert's kingship and decided on the issue of succession. As this was the year of Bannockburn we can clearly see that the risks to Sir Neil were still very real. Such uncommon bravery and loyalty demands an uncommon reward and this was given in the form of the King's sister, Lady Marjory Bruce – a gesture that was a serious mark of a King's regard. As well as marriage into the Royal family he was granted several lands forfeited by followers of Balliol.

Sir Neil's son, John, was the first Campbell to be made an Earl, having received the confiscated lands of Atholl. His older brother Sir Colin Og (Young Colin) became Lord of Lochow on the death of Sir Neil in 1316. Colin joined Edward Bruce in the ill-fated Scottish campaign in Ireland. There he so distinguished himself that additional lands in Argyle were granted in recognition of his gallantry. During the usurpation of the Scots throne by the Balliols in the 1330s it was Colin Og who stormed and took Dunoon Castle, which was then garrisoned by the English. In a foretaste of Dunaverty, three centuries in the future, Sir Colin executed every member of the garrison, although, as we have seen, such an action was not at all unusual.

The acts of valour and loyalty of Clan Campbell could fill many books on their own. The men who followed Sir Colin appear to have been as energetic and successful as their predecessors in expanding the power and territory of their clan. It is sometimes difficult to follow who did what as the stories are an exciting mix of truth and legend. It also clouds their story that, with the exception of Sir Duncan, who was made Lord Campbell in 1445, all clan chiefs were either called Archibald or Colin, until the 2nd Duke, John in the 18th century.

We can take Duncan as fairly representative of the Clan Chiefs. King James the First had become a prisoner of the English in 1406, and while the young sovereign was held in captivity the Duke of Albany ruled Scotland as Regent. Albany appears to have been quite happy to leave matters as they were and made no serious effort to have the King ransomed. It appears, though, that Sir Duncan Campbell made strenuous efforts to have him released.

There are two versions of the events surrounding the release of James. In one, Sir Duncan prevails upon the Duke of Albany to pay a ransom to the English for the release of the King. In another, overtures to the English are left until Albany has died, but Sir Duncan is one of the nobles who carries the ransom south. In either case, Sir Duncan was notable for his loyalty to the King and James did not forget this. In the fullness of time Duncan was made a member of the Privy Council, Justice-General and Lieutenant of Argyle. Possibly from this latter title he was the first Campbell to use Argyle rather than Lochow to describe his possessions.

After King James returned in 1424 he set about rooting out potential traitors, one of whom was a MacDonald chief. The man sent to interrogate the chief was a Campbell, but his precise identity and relationship to Sir Duncan is unknown. Whoever he was, the meeting progressed badly and Campbell attempted to arrest MacDonald, but a fight ensued, culminating in the death of MacDonald. As with so many things in this area, the details are cloudy and indistinct. It may not have been the particular issue that made the MacDonalds and Campbells such bitter enemies, but it certainly helped the process along.

From Duncan onwards the Campbell chiefs set about a process of consolidating their often widely dispersed lands. Demonstrably capable of waging war with their neighbours, the Campbells were also ready to use diplomacy, persuasion or even the courts to further their aims. Another factor that worked in their favour was the lure of their name. Campbell is, even today, one of the most common surnames, and great numbers of those who carry the name have no ancestral link with Clan Duihne. Many come from clans that were absorbed or conquered by the Campbells, but some simply assumed the surname at some point in the past. In this the Campbells were unique among the Highlanders; good, rational commonsense was always preferred to romantic notions of heritage and fairytales about descent from legendary kings and Celtic Gods.

Another factor that was of immense assistance to the Campbells was that all branches of the clan were perfectly willing to accept the Lords of Lochow as clan chiefs. It should be said, though, that one branch alone, the MacArthur Campbells of Strachur, always contended that they were the true descendants of Diarmid O'Duihne. If we accept that Archibald was a member of a lower clan when he married Eva, then there may be some justification for the Strachur position. However, the claim is a millennium old, and no other Campbells ever supported their position.

Sir Duncan was succeeded by his grandson, another Colin, who was created the first Earl of Argyll in 1457. To grasp any sense of just how long ago these events took place, it may be useful to consider that the Turks had only finally destroyed the Roman Empire four years before Colin became an Earl. We tend to think of the ancient world as belonging to the realms of thousands of years ago. It is actually considerably closer than might be thought.

From the start of this book I was warned that any attempt to write about a specific part of Scotland was doomed to be drawn into the larger history of Scotland itself, specifically the 'official' history with its southern and Edinburgh focus. The pressure described has indeed been experienced, but never more so than in this chapter about the Campbells, and it is precisely the affinity of the Campbells to the rulers of Scotland that has created this situation.

No other clan has ever been so closely identified with the Scottish crown. In this the Campbells were not always consciously pursuing the policies of the King. It just so happened that, time after time, the needs of the clan were on a parallel with those of its monarch. It was this that eventually led to Campbell supremacy over their great rival, Clan MacDonald.

In any kingdom, the most natural course of action would seem to be that of following the monarch, where that ruler is accepted and legally established. In some respects it is incomprehensible that the MacDonalds should be so well regarded when so many of their activities were designed to promote ambitions that were completely at odds with the aims of their king. This clan never saw the Scottish Crown as anything other than a tax-gathering nuisance, and it did not waken up to just how powerful the King might be until it was too late.

We have studied some of the notable and admirable characters in the history of Clan Campbell, but it would do its great history no service if the Massacre of Glencoe were ignored. The Campbell involvement in an earlier, less well-known, atrocity at Dunaverty will be covered in a later chapter. At Glencoe the Campbells were acting as government officers, though an inevitable consequence of the family's close relationship with the Crown was that the darker aspects of state policy might taint it.

King James II of England and VII of Scots was deposed on December 11, 1688, after a monstrous three years on the throne of the combined realms. This cruel and vindictive creature was a Roman Catholic, but his Christianity was of the rabid and intolerant variety. He was blindly determined that the Roman faith would be restored to his Kingdoms of Scotland, England and Ireland, and set about a relentless persecution of the Covenanters (later called Presbyterians).

Neither Scotland nor England wanted a Catholic king, and little time passed from James' accession on February 6, 1685 until the Earl of Argyle, at this time in exile, invaded Scotland in May. A few weeks later the Duke of Monmouth, another political exile, landed at Lyme Regis. On June 11, 1685 he was proclaimed the true James II of England. Both men were confident of massed support against James but both were to be sorely disappointed. Very few Scots or English joined their banners, indeed even the Campbells did not support Argyle, and the rebellion was quickly put down. Both men were summarily executed within weeks and from then on James embarked on a reign of terror.

For three years this tyrant pursued the bloody pursuit of restoring the Roman faith. His utter disregard for Parliament and his relentless determination to destroy the Churches of Scotland and England eventually provoked his enemies to action. The Immortal Seven were the Bishop of London and six supporters, who sent an invitation to James' son-in-law, William of Orange, to protect his wife, Mary's succession to the throne. This pretext had been arrived at with the birth of James' son, also called James. The arrival of this child, who would be raised as a Roman Catholic, and would be heir to the thrones of Scotland and England, was too much for James' enemies. Until then James' heir was his daughter Mary, who was a Protestant, and it was the likelihood of her succession that had protected James until the birth of his son.

In November 1688 William of Orange landed in England. James made a show of resistance but in the end he was abandoned by practically everyone, including his younger daughter, Anne. He was captured, but more or less permitted to escape to exile in France. On February 13, 1689 William III of England and II of Scots was crowned jointly with his wife, Mary II of England and Scots, the daughter of James II. This joint rule was very uncommon; the last time two monarchs shared rule was in the 11th century in Scotland and the 9th century in England. The reason for it appears to be that William was not prepared to simply assume the role of Prince Consort to Queen Mary. At the same time Mary was uncomfortable with the thought of ruling alone. She had prepared to be Queen, but had assumed it would be on the death of her father. The thought that she had deposed him sat heavily with her.

William's accession was not complete, though. He and Mary were now undisputed rulers of England and Scotland. The English took the view that James had legally abdicated by fleeing the country, while the Scots regarded his actions against their kingdom as effectively forfeiting his right to rule. In addition to this James had never actually been crowned King of Scots. The fact that no future British ruler would be either could not have been anticipated at the time. In Ireland, James II was still King and it was this that left William and Mary's rule incomplete.

In 1690 William went to Ireland to join his troops and, at the Battle of the Boyne, James was finally defeated. He again fled to France where he continued to plot his return, but it was not to be. It is always an interesting pursuit, to consider how history might have turned out had certain alternatives occurred – interesting but generally inconclusive. In the case of James II there can be absolutely no doubt that his continued rule would have been a catastrophe for Scotland and England. The Scots Stewart dynasty had been expelled and few Scots or English lamented its passing.

In 1691 the Irish attempted a revolt but were again beaten by William's army. The apparent ease with which he handled Ireland was not to be repeated in the Scottish Highlands. As stated above, most Scots were determinedly opposed to James, but in the largely Catholic Highlands he continued to have considerable support among the clans. William had no time for this, and the clans were given an ultimatum in 1691. By January 1, 1692 all were to have sworn allegiance to William and Mary or face the consequences.

On December 30, 1691 Alexander MacIan MacDonald, head of the MacDonalds of Glencoe, started out for Fort William to make the necessary oath. On arrival he was advised that he was at the wrong place and he was sent south to Inveraray. The weather was terrible and this led to him turning up two days late. To compound this he was kept waiting for a further three days until being allowed to swear his allegiance to King William and Queen Mary. Despite missing the deadline it was plain to anyone that this old man had striven to fulfil the Royal command. Alexander thought he was now safe and returned to Glencoe.

The decision to make an example of the MacDonalds of Glencoe seems strange considering that their chief had made such strenuous efforts to fulfil his commitments. The truth was that a force had already been stationed at Fort William, and the government was determined to 'root out that damnable sept'. The MacDonalds' fate had been sealed well before Alexander missed his appointment.

Campbell histories have never disputed the massacre, but a point that has been emphasised is that the Earl of Argyle had nothing to do with it. There is no doubt that this is true. The perpetrator of the deed was one Captain Robert Campbell of Glenlyon, a gambler and a drunkard who would eventually die a pauper. The decision to act against the MacDonalds of Glencoe, though, was made by Sir John Campbell of Glenorchy, Earl of Breadalbane. These two Campbells only became involved after the decision to act had already been made by the Secretary of State, Sir John Dalrymple of Stair, and after the King himself had countersigned the order.

On February 1 two advanced units were sent into Glencoe under Captain Campbell, where they received the hospitality of the MacDonalds and were billeted around many homes. On February 12 Campbell received his orders from Lieutenant-Colonel Hamilton and Major Duncanson, who had jointly planned the actual massacre that was to come. At 5am every MacDonald under the age of 70 was to be butchered.

The task facing Campbell was not as easy as it might seem: he had only 120 men at his disposal against several hundred MacDonalds, it was still the middle of the night, and the weather was appalling. Reinforcements under Colonel Hamilton and Major Duncanson did not arrive, and it has been suggested that this delay was deliberate to allow these officers to plead innocence. On top of this is a tradition in Argyll that some of the billeted troops warned the MacDonalds of what was to happen.

The end result was that the massacre was a disaster. Only 38 MacDonalds were murdered while hundreds escaped into the surrounding hills. Many of these must have died of exposure, but overall the botched execution of the King's order spared numerous other clan members.

The massacre was quickly made public in Scotland, and the outrage it provoked was as intense then as the memory of the act is in modern times. It is plain from this that there is more to an atrocity than simply the number of victims. In the 16th century the Earl of Essex was responsible for a massacre on Rathlin Island that took the lives of 600 men, women and children, but this slaughter is hardly recognised today. The deaths of 38 MacDonalds at Glencoe is known the world over, and it seems to be a mixture of elements attaching to it that makes the massacre so potent: the breach of Highland hospitality; the involvement of the Campbells, centuries-old enemies of the Macdonalds; the blatant disregard for Alexander's attempt to make his oath; the presence of a force ready to act regardless of the oath being taken or not; the wickedness of its planning, and the cold-blooded treachery of its execution.

To the above list has to be added the deliberate sanction of the State. This was no covert operation carried out by William's clandestine agents. This was a Royal Order and it is with the King that responsibility stops. William knew this and attempted to restore his good image by ordering a public inquiry three years after the act. At this inquiry the 'perpetrators' were brought to justice, but ultimately only reprimands were handed out. This tends to support the King's awareness of his own culpability. William was not a bad man. He was dull, unlikeable and bad-tempered, but not bad. There was no way that he would punish those who had only been acting on his orders.

Returning to the Campbells, it now becomes difficult to understand how they have become so closely associated with this terrible deed. As we have seen, the King, on the guidance of the Secretary of State, ordered the massacre. Colonel Hamilton and Major Duncanson planned the details of the action, and of the 120 troops who took part in the massacre, more than 100 were not Campbells.

It is true that a Campbell selected the MacDonalds of Glencoe and another Campbell led the small advanced force, but these two men and the dozen or so Campbell troops who entered Glencoe were hardly representative of the force arrayed against the MacDonalds that night. The blame lay with the King, and it has to be concluded that the dark reputation acquired by the Campbells after Glencoe is undeserved. Perhaps it was a later realisation that the massacre was the final bloody act in the turbulent history of Clan MacDonald. Considered this way, it was quite natural to look for the clan's ancient enemy, the Campbells, and there they were, numbered among the Government troops, just as they had been time and again over the preceding centuries. The fact that they were represented in no significantly greater numbers than any other family was disregarded, and time and the failure of memory did the rest. Within a few years, a Government sponsored massacre was turned into the last brutal act of the ascendant Campbells against their ancient and declining enemy, the MacDonalds.

It was during the reign of King William and Queen Mary that the Earls of Argyle were elevated to Dukes. This was achieved by the 10th Earl who proved, in the time honoured Campbell way, that he was a thoroughly reliable adviser and subject. The 2nd Duke was a key player in pushing the Act of Union through the Scottish Parliament in 1707. It should be pointed out though that he also voted in 1713 to have the Union dissolved again, but this motion was defeated. Despite falling from favour for a time he was eventually later elevated from Earl to Duke of Greenwich.

The Campbells remain the Dukes of Argyll to this day and the Duke is still held to be the Clan Chief, the son of the Great Colin. The present chapter has dealt mainly with this House but, in closing, it should be pointed out that there are several other current and historic Houses, one of the reasons that the Campbell name is so widely used. These Houses are: Craignish, Breadalbane, Cawdor, Loudon, Lochnell, Asknish, Auchinbreck and Aberuchill. There are others but these are small.

As a final note regarding the surname itself, it has been suggested that the origin of the name Campbell is from the Gaelic words *Cam* for crooked and *Beal* for mouth. This is highly unlikely and probably originates from some ancient insult that gained some credence and was eventually regarded as representing some facial feature of Diarmid O'Duihne. It may be concluded from this chapter that the many enemies of Clan Campbell would doubtless delight in their description as crooked mouthed but, even it were true, it is a charge that they are no more deserving of than any other ancient Scots family.

Gigha

Lying only two and a half kilometres from Rhunahaorine Point on the Kintyre mainland is the Isle of Gigha. Ten kilometres long and three at its widest, it is almost a miniature version of Scotland; from its rocky, coarse north through the hills and high fields of the centre to the lush green farms of the south. This beautiful place sits in a wide expanse of ocean, surrounded by Ireland, Islay, Jura, Scarba, Knapdale and Kintyre. The only visible gaps in these walls of land are to the south-west, into the Atlantic Ocean, and to the south, through the North Channel and into the Irish Sea. Sitting deep within Dalriada and occupying a strategically important location, it is strange that this island has been forgotten even more completely than Dalriada and Argyll.

Two things immediately mitigate against a clear understanding of Gigha's history. The first is the small (if admirable) scale of archaeological study, and the second is the lack of a local historical tradition. In both of these Gigha suffers simply because of its remoteness and size. Sites on the mainland of Scotland, closer to the great centres, obviously receive greater attention than remote places, and the historical awareness of most local Gigha people is certainly no worse than in any other part of Scotland. Unfortunately, again, areas close to the great centres do not require a local interest as plenty comes from the world of academia and popular historical study. A great deal, therefore, has to be conjectured from the little that is available, but the first thing that suggests an ancient importance for Gigha is its location.

Centrally placed, within a body of water that could be mistaken for a vast inland loch, Gigha is impossible to miss. Heading south from Tarbert it can be seen initially at the distant end of West Loch Tarbert. After a few kilometres it dominates the ocean to the west of the road, which follows the coast down Kintyre. Even from the south of Kintyre, at Machrihanish, it can be seen far to the north quite clearly. The thought that this obvious landmass could have been studiously ignored by wave after wave of invaders, immigrants and travellers, millennium after millennium is absurd.

Recent research has shown that the sea route from Ireland to Iona was probably not in the Atlantic – to the west of Islay and Jura – as was previously thought. Such a route was always regarded as frighteningly risky, and while it did much to enhance our sense of the bravery of the men who made the trip, their sanity had to be occasionally questioned as well. The new evidence suggests convincingly that travellers instead made their way north from Ireland, past Gigha to the east, and on to Jura's eastern shore. There the boats were dragged 1,000 metres or so across land to Loch Tarbert in the west. They then journeyed out from Jura, past Colonsay to the west, and on to Iona; a slower but infinitely safer route with much land on all sides to run for in the event of difficulties. By comparison the Atlantic route is simply too fraught with potential problems.

The research has not focussed on Gigha, but it is not hard to speculate that travellers may have found it expedient at times to run with the prevailing south-westerly winds and stop over on Gigha before sailing on to Jura. There was no need in those far off days, for people to make the Ireland to Iona trip at breakneck speed. A safe, measured journey from Ireland to Iona via Gigha, Jura and Colonsay would only have taken a few days, but a trip out into the Atlantic with only land to the east and the prevailing winds pushing their light craft towards this might never be completed at all.

A major reason for the view that Gigha was never regarded as of any consequence was touched upon in an earlier chapter. At the present day, Kintyre is the far end of Scotland. Gigha is less than a hundred kilometres from Glasgow, as the crow flies, but in the Scottish mind it is a part of the wild and remote Highlands. This is the inevitable consequence of the policy, begun long ago by Malcolm Canmore, of turning the focus of Scots policy away from the north. The Highlands and Islands became Edinburgh's remote back door. When the capital became London this remoteness became acute and very physically real.

Add to this physical distance a vague mental conception by the Lowlands and England and we have a place on the map where dragons once dwelled.

Before Canmore the Hebrides, the Highlands and Ulster were areas bound closely together by trade and by blood. These ties continued into the 20th century but by that time they had been virtually diluted into extinction. It is a mark of how strong they once were, though, that they survived so long. In the early 19th century it was common for fishermen from Ireland to pull small boats onto the sands across from Craro Island on Gigha's west shore and climb the short distance up to Moinean Sitheil, close to Achamore Farm. At the top of the hill they paid their respects to two small stones called the Bodach and the Cailleach, the *Old Ones of Gigha*

The Bodach and the Cailleach are tiny objects, and are something of a shock to a visitor more used to finding great slabs of stone and mysterious stone circles. Their alleged power, however, is not to be sniffed at for these stones supposedly stand an ancient vigil which preserves the fertility and prosperity of the island. As well as the Irish fishermen, the locals once made offerings of food and drink at this spot. Here, straight away, we have a link between cultures that are today profoundly separate from one another.

For many centuries, the Irish were said to have come to Gigha on a pilgrimage to the Cladh an Righ (the King's Grave). This monolith, which lies on the slopes above East Tarbert Bay, is reputed to be the burial place of a mighty chieftain, and the visiting Irish came to pay their respects to him. Whoever this great man was is less important than the clear fact that there were strong and enduring links between Ireland and Gigha.

Until the early 19th century, the Irish, as well as locals and others, were also in the habit of visiting Tobar a Bheathaig (The Well of Beathag). This well is on Cnoc Largie, the same hill as the King's Grave, and was supposed to have magic and healing powers. Its mystique involved having the ability to shift the winds to more favourable directions. For a small offering to the aged local lady who tended the well, a short ceremony would be undertaken and, it is recorded, the wind never failed to shift as requested. It was also known as the Tobar Mor (The Great Well) because of its reliable cures and miracles.

From ancient times, when the above shows of respect originated, until the 18th century the residents of Gigha and those of Antrim would have spoken practically the same language. In religion, too, they had a common heritage until the Reformation split the Western Christian world. Even after this, though, ancient pre-Christian beliefs were secretly maintained and it was these that were being exercised when Roman Catholic Ulster fishermen and Protestant Gigha farmers made their separate visits to the *Old Ones.*

So why would fishermen, at a distance from home, go to the trouble of undertaking these pilgrimages? Clearly there was more to Gigha in their minds and memories than just an agricultural backwater, at the fringes of Great Britain. In the first place, it would not have been a backwater. It sits at the heart of the world the fisherman knew, and islands have always held an important spiritual place in the hearts of Celtic peoples. All through the islands of Dalriada are chapels and shrines, the most famous of which is Iona, far to the north. Gigha is accessible to Ireland and its name, at least its Norse name, may explain its importance.

Its Norse lords knew Gigha as Gudey, which has been translated as *Good Island* or *God's Island.* Most researchers favour the latter but, if it is the correct translation, then we have to explain why God would be so explicitly linked to one island rather than another. That it is beautiful cannot be doubted, but it is hardly more beautiful than the Kintyre mainland opposite. An answer may be that the island, at some point in its past, had profound spiritual importance to the inhabitants of the surrounding lands. If we assume that the Vikings simply translated the existing island name into their own language then Gigha's religious importance dates to the early years of Dalriada and possibly even earlier.

At some point Gudey became Gigha. It is doubtful that this was a reversion to its original name since the word Gigha has no meaningful Gaelic or Brythonic translation. If it had followed the normal process of names mutating into Gaelic then it would have become Gudhaidh, rather than Gicgha. My own, unsupported, opinion on this matter is that Gudey was, at some date during Norse rule, given the name of an individual. In modern Icelandic there is a name, Gigja, which is likely to have been available to the Norse lords of the Sudreys during their period of rule. Indeed, a perusal of the genealogies of Clan MacDonald, once the Lords of the Isles, shows this very name among its many modern descendants. Whilst this is speculative, the use of proper names for places is very common, and naming important locations after honoured individuals is even more common. Taking an existing place name, such as Gudey, and replacing it with a meaningless word is not common at all. Whether we will ever know who this Gigja was is doubtful, but, whoever the name was given to, they, in turn, gave it to three places in the Sudreys; the Gigha of this chapter, Gigha of Barra and Drumgigha in Mull.

Another aspect of modern Gigha, which has unfortunately tended to support the view that it is of little historical importance, is its tiny population. At the start of the 21st century this stands at a little over 100, with the bulk of this population in the southern half of the island. This was not always the case and, in 1792, the population was recorded as 614. In the 17th century, the northern part of Gigha was considerably more important, and the laird's house was located only a kilometre from Port Righ (The King's Port) at the northernmost point of the island. This 'king' would have been a tribal leader along the Dalriadan and Pictish model, in effect a sub-king, but the presence of such an important leader again drags us from a complacent view that this island never had any serious importance. A population six times larger than today's, a laird's residence in a later depopulated area and a Royal landing point are suggestive of a place of no small significance.

The poor size of the modern population has caused much concern and it is certainly true that a community requires a certain number of people to ensure its long-term survival. The number stands up well against the 1931 census, though, which recorded 210 people living on Gigha. This was before the movement of young people in particular from rural to urban areas had become the steady haemorrhage that we witness today. A part of the equation that is often neglected, however, is that a steady stream of incomers goes some way to stopping the situation from becoming fatal. It is true that these people are generally older than those who are leaving, and they are fewer in number, but it is still a little early to give up on Gigha and, indeed, Argyll.

Returning to more populated, if not necessarily more prosperous times, the founding of Alban Dalriada was traditionally dated to 498 AD. There is absolutely no doubt that Gigha (whatever it was then called) became an early part of the new Scots Kingdom. The ruined church on the island at Kilchattan is St Cathan's, and this Saint is believed to have accompanied St Kieran to Alban Dalriada in 536 AD. From this it is assumed that St Cathan arrived on Gigha in the very earliest years of the Scots Kingdom, and nearly 30 years before St Columba founded Iona.

The ruined church is 13th century, but tradition states that it was built on the site of St Cathan's cell on Gigha. St Cathan was based on Bute, from which island he moved about Kintyre and the closer islands, spreading his message. There is no tradition of a building occupying the site prior to the construction of the church, but there is a legend concerning a holy well. A well still exists close to the church, but it was covered over some years ago when the adjacent road was strengthened to permit use by trucks. Given that Christian churches were often built on the site of previously Pagan religious places it is quite possible that St Cathan chose the location for his cell at a place holding some importance to the contemporary islanders.

We cannot be certain exactly what St Cathan built on Gigha but any debate really revolves around whether it was a chapel or simply accommodation for him on his travels. I tend to think that, if he was using an existing holy place, in a place that was not yet firmly within the rule of the Church, then Kilchattan would have been something of both, but small and unassuming. The role of these Saints, who bravely took their message around potentially hostile lands, was to teach and persuade and then to convert. The obscene forced conversions of later centuries would have horrified these pious, strong men. Nothing was to be gained by violating existing holy places and it was from one of these that St Cathan presented himself to the islanders and welcomed them to hear the word.

Given the general neglect of Argyll history the importance of these men may be questioned, but we only have to move forward a few years to the time of St Columba to see where their efforts led. If it had not been for the likes of St Cathan and his brothers, preaching in places like Gigha and extending the rule of the Celtic Church, then Columba would not have had the necessary Dalriadan base to begin his great work. We should not forget that his calling involved not only the evangelisation of Scotland but also a large portion of England as well. By the time of Columba, barely 30 years after Cathan, Kintyre and the islands had been thoroughly visited and, where appropriate, settled by Saints of the Celtic Church.

On Cara, Gigha's diminutive southern partner, is another small chapel. In 1700 this was recorded as Cella Sanctissimae Trinitatis (The Cell of the Most Holy Trinity). The fact that this religious structure was not named after any particular saint suggests that its pre-mediaeval predecessor was not a chapel as such, but rather a retreat for the clergy of Kintyre and the surrounding isles. From this we can build a picture of a mission spread throughout Argyll and the islands, with small chapels and cells in many locations and a smaller number of retreats for the Saints to rest and reinvigorate themselves.

So what sort of a world was this young Dalriada, only recently set out on its independent way from its Irish namesake? Until relatively recently the historical view was that the Dalriadic Scots set foot ashore on Kintyre and then proceeded to demolish Pictish power throughout what is now Argyll. A picturesque theory certainly, but, as was demonstrated in earlier chapers, patently absurd. What is altogether more likely is that the Picts were, in the early years of the 6th century, embroiled in costly wars between their various families. When Fergus the Great founded his dynasty in Kintyre and Argyll he probably did so as the result of negotiations with neighbouring Pictish lords. There is no evidence to support the earlier theory that the Scots practically stormed the Kintyre beaches.

Gigha then came under Scots control, having been a Pictish island, and the change of lord need not have been anything but peaceful. Again, earlier suggestions that the Picts of Gigha were taken into slavery are unlikely. When St Cathan and St Columba began their travels, it was through a stable and civilised nation. That is not to say that there were no dangers. Many would have harboured a lasting bitterness at their change of masters and, on top of this, the message being carried by these Scots Saints would have been less than welcome in some quarters because the Picts were, at this time, still Pagan.

King Fergus of Alban Dalriada, including Gigha, met St Patrick while he was a young man at his father's court in Irish Dalriada. St Patrick is said to have prophesied that he would become the father of a nation. This, of course, came to pass, but Fergus enjoyed his kingship for only three years until he died in 501 AD. His son, Domangart, an old man himself, ruled until 507 but *his* son, Comgall, ruled Dalriada for 31 years. This remarkable reign took in the period of St Cathan's arrival, and it is clear that Comgall managed to find a successful formula for living with the Picts in the north and the Britons across the Clyde Estuary.

After Comgall came Gabrain, from whom the Clan of that name sprang. He was a vigorous warrior king who attempted to push the Scots Kingdom into Pictish territories. He had some success in this regard, but it was not to be permanent. At his death in 558 Dalriada occupied just the same territories as when he had succeeded his brother.

After Gabrain came his nephew, Conall, son of Comgall. This king had none of his uncle's aggressive instincts and sought alternative methods of securing peace amongst the Scots, the Picts and the Britons. It was this Scots King who welcomed his kinsman, St Columba, in 563 and gifted him the island of Iona. Conall saw in Columba, who was also a candidate for election to the High Kingship of Ireland, a powerful ally, but, more importantly, a possible route to the peace he sought.

Such were the political routes that finally brought Columba to Iona. The charming story of his desire to establish his community beyond the sight of Ireland is almost certainly a fiction. The real Columba was a tough, resourceful warrior as well as a Royal Prince and a priest. As stated before, Columba's mission was made a little easier by the earlier efforts of men such as St Cathan and St Kieran. Their activities around Kintyre made a community as far north as Iona a viable proposition and Iona was precisely where King Conall needed his new ally to be. From this island, right next to Mull, an island divided between the Scots and Picts, Columba could continue to spread the Christian message into Pictland.

The importance of St Cathan cannot be overstated but that comment should be qualified by saying that he was no more important than any other of his brave counterparts. The importance of Gigha to St Cathan can be demonstrated by the presence there of a church dedicated to him. This is not to say that Gigha deserves any special mention concerning the spread of Christianity through the young Kingdom of Dalriada, and then into the older Pictland. What it does deserve, though, is at least the same degree of mention as any other place in Argyll from which the new religion spread its civilising influence.

The Western Isles of Scotland were the Southern Isles of Norway, and by a long and relentless process they finally all fell under the authority of the Norse King. The advent of the Vikings was a terrifying episode in the history of Britain and Ireland. This is not to say that this enemy always routed the Scots. In 987 the Vikings were defeated at a great battle and 350 of their number, who had been involved in an attack on Iona the preceding year, were executed.

Iona was a regular target for Viking aggression and we can assume that this was a matter of policy. Iona was a place of deep religious significance to the Scots Kingdom, and the Vikings were well aware of this. There is no evidence that other religious centres were subjected to such intense ferocity, although they were by no means treated lightly, and it is plain that the Vikings saw the annihilation of Iona as the key to breaking the Scots will.

As things transpired Iona was repaired after each attack; that is five times between 794 and 986, and the early dominion of the Vikings extended only to the northern isles. Kintyre was only secured in the 11th century, by which time the Vikings had become Christians. This did not mean that their fighting prowess was in any way diminished, but their legendary barbarity was tempered to a great extent. Their conversion occurred at some time during their slow progress south and by the time they reached Gigha their entire world view was radically altered from that of their raiding ancestors.

There is little doubt that the natives of Gigha were placed under some degree of serfdom by their Norse lords, but it is likely that there was no serious reduction in their living standards or their status. The major initial change was simply one of masters. As Christians themselves, the new Norse lords took great care not to interfere with the established Columban Church. The Icelandic Sagas refer to the island as Gudey, the name given to it by the new masters. Again we come back to this name and another possibility is that the name was chosen by the now Christian Norsemen as a display of reverence for priests who were still working from the island in the same cause established by St Cathan. Even if this is not the case, the decision to change its name in the first place points to a spiritual importance for Gigha that was still powerful.

For a time Gigha would have been the most remote of the Sudreys (if we ignore Man), but in time Kintyre, Arran and Bute became Norse possessions and Gigha was now in a more central position with regard to the most southerly islands. It is this strategic location that supports the vague historical references to there being a Tynwald Hill on the island. This name still exists in the Isle of Man where, every year, the two legislative bodies meet in joint session on Tynwald Hill as the Court of Tynwald. Still a proper legal procedure, the meeting has nowadays assumed a certain ceremonial air, but it is precisely the sort of business that would have been transacted on Gigha while it was a Norse possession. The major difference is that, whilst the Isle of Man is a sovereign state subject to the modern British Crown, Gigha's Tynwald would have been more of a provincial parliament, but with jurisdiction over the neighbouring mainland. Another Tynwald is recorded as having existed on Islay which, when it is given proper consideration, makes perfect sense. The Norse authority extended over a vast maritime empire and the King's Law would require several local centres to be administered properly.

The location of this Tynwald Hill has been given as a field between North Drumachro Farm (now a private home, Drumallan) and the island's main road. It has been suggested that there never was a Tynwald Hill on the island, and that the story grew from confusion over a tribal meeting place below St Cathan's Church and a little distance from the alleged site. This is perfectly understandable, given the incomplete history of the island, but the presence of other features in the same field, close to Drumallan, lends weight to the story.

An access path runs east from the main road for 300 metres, where there is a turning north towards Drumallan. Immediately to the west of this northward path are three prominent rises, all in the same field as, and to the east of the alleged Tynwald Hill. The northernmost is substantial and, looking out over Ardminish Bay as it does, has to be the site of an ancient fort or lookout position. The southernmost mound looks artificial but is, in all probability, simply an overgrown plug of rock. There is some indication of ancient quarrying activity on its western side. The central mound is also clearly artificial but it is considerably more than a mound of rubble.

Locally this central mound was called Haakon's Hillock until quite recently. After the Battle of Largs in 1263, Haakon's fleet headed for home, stopping off initially at the nearest provincial centre, Gigha. There his dead were taken ashore and laid to rest in a single mass grave, over which was raised a sizeable mound of rocks and earth. The location of the burial may have been symbolic, close to the seat of local authority. Some authorities have dismissed this story, of the massed burial, but it makes much more sense for a Christian warlord to bury his dead rather than simply tip them over the sides of his vessels. The Norse force was under no pressure as it retreated and Gigha was the first completely safe landfall outside of the Clyde Estuary. The Scots had repulsed the enemy and left it at that. Indeed, it would be several years before the Norse possessions were ceded *by treaty* to the Scots Crown.

In denying the existence of the Tynwald Hill on Gigha, one authority goes on to describe the fort over Ardminish Bay in some detail. His conclusion is that this location was more likely to have been a seat of the authority of a chief. So the Tynwald may, in fact, have been 100 metres to the east, overlooking the bay. Whatever the truth, the field to the west of Drumallan contains several very interesting features. Only an excavation at the central hillock, though, will prove beyond doubt that it is a mass grave. Whatever it is, though, a discussion with one of the islanders uncovered a curious fact: as a child, whilst she and her friends were quite content to play around the fort/chief's-seat location above the shore, none of them would go near the central mound. It has also been suggested that grazing sheep seem to shun the spot as well.

A related local legend states that a Viking longship is buried somewhere on the island and the likeliest location would seem to be this central mound. While investigating the mound, I had my attention drawn to a very distinct outline in the field around it. To the south was the clear shape of the bow of a ship. To the north the 'stern' curved close to the mound. After the initial shock it had to be concluded that all we were looking at was the result of centuries of planting and ploughing leaving a particular shape on the ground. In any case the shape is quite unlike a longship.

The Saga of Haakon, which describes the Battle of Largs, also provides a small detail that quite inadvertently supports the view that Gigha held a position of some importance among the Norse possessions. Prior to the Battle of Largs Haakon collected the bulk of his fleet at Gigha, which he made his headquarters. The reason given for this in the Saga is that from Gigha he could command both the mainland of Kintyre and the islands of Islay and Jura. If this tactical position was identified in 1263, then it was certainly known long before that date.

Another small detail deserves to be mentioned; very little doubt has been cast on the fact that the fleet anchored between Gigalum and Gigha. This natural harbour is sheltered and the water is deep. The main road from the south to the north of the island also accesses the area. It seems unlikely that King Haakon and his predecessors would have found Gigha's anchorage so convenient, but would not have found it expedient to establish some sort of permanent official presence there. It is not possible to have it both ways: Gigha can not have been an unimportant backwater while at the same time possessing a harbour that the Norse King naturally turned to when he needed. It may not have been a great centre but there is little doubt that it was important.

Coming forward to the 21st Century the question may well be asked: if this little place was important in its history, does it have any worth now, beyond the interests of its own people? As with all issues, historical or current, it depends on your particular interest but recently this forgotten speck within a forgotten corner of Britain has come to the attention of all of the British peoples. The issue was one of Land Reform but the arguments go all the way back to the early days of Dalriada.

Gigha is a Barony, and this title equates to land ownership, but not in the strict sense any homeowner is familiar with today. On Gigha, ownership of the land went hand in hand with ownership of the community itself. In the hands of a good laird a community such as Gigha can be expected to thrive, but by the end of the 20th century it had become politically unacceptable that the fate of allegedly free people rested in the hands of a single property owner. This issue became increasingly prominent when the island passed from the hands of individuals and into the ownership of corporations that existed for the sole purpose of making profit.

It is not the purpose of this book to argue the rights and wrongs of private land ownership, but it needs to be said that with possession of a community comes responsibility, and responsibility is something that corporations have shown a frightening disregard for, particularly in recent years. Corporate bodies exist to generate money, and this has proven to be an admirable, if volatile, method of expanding the wealth of nations that subscribe to the ideals. Unfortunately, in a community situation, the local people become a variable that simply does not fit squarely onto a balance sheet.

In 2001 the community on Gigha purchased the estate from the corporate owner, with assistance from the new Scottish Parliament. It goes without saying that there have been issues arising from this acquisition, but what has happened is historic and it is fitting that a place like Gigha should be one of the instruments in the final dismantling of the Feudal System in Scotland. This forgotten island, in a forgotten corner of Scotland has helped tear down a system that was foisted on an unwilling Scotland centuries ago. It is quite telling that Scotland, one of the last nations in Europe to adopt feudalism, was the only one, at the turn of the 21st century, to still have it enshrined in its statutes.

To paraphrase an islander who was interviewed on national television: "We are the last serfs in Europe." Whatever the future holds, that scathing indictment will never again be aired on Gigha.

St Columba

After the death of King Conall in 574, his cousin Aedan MacGabrain assumed the throne of Dalriada. As his surname immediately shows, he was the son of the mighty Gabrain, and he appears to have had a lot of his father's military skills, for he set out to retake the Pictish lands held briefly by Gabrain. By the laws of succession as they were at that time, Aedan had a lesser claim to the throne than Conall's son and his own brother who were both perfectly eligible to become King, but, as has been demonstrated before, there was no clear cut rule that automatically excluded him so the matter became a serious dispute within the Royal family.

Before the dispute came to bloodshed it was agreed that St Columba would consider the various claimants and provide a binding decision. Columba thought long and hard and for most of his deliberations he favoured Aedan's brother, Eoganan. This man was a peaceful soul and very well educated, just the sort of leader Dalriada needed, or so thought Columba. Unfortunately the Lord plainly had different plans, for Columba was subjected to a powerful vision where he was being brutally whipped by an angel who declared that Aedan was the rightful successor to the throne.

St Columba made his decision in favour of Aedan, probably without realising its full significance. This was the first time that a Christian King was selected and ordained by God and it would become the basis for the Stewart dynasty's belief in the Divine Appointment of Kings, a belief that was to have catastrophic consequences for Britain more than 1,000 years later. As it turned out, at this early date, the choice of Aedan was just what Alban Dalriada needed. We will, however, return to this.

As was explored in the chapter on Gigha, the Dalriadan Church was sufficiently well established by 498 that it was able to send missionaries across the North Channel to Kintyre and there begin a slow and relentless campaign of conversion. Clearly St Columba was not around in the late 5th century to be a part of the process that would set the Celtic Church on such solid foundations, but his predecessors were every bit as talented, devout and tenacious, as he would prove to be a century on.

The great apostle of Irish Dalriada was a young man called Patrick, who was kidnapped by the Scots from his home in southern Britain. We should be clear here that, prior to 498, the term Scots applies only to the people of Dalriada in Ireland. After this date it will be specified which of the Scots communities is being referred to. Patrick was taken to Dalriada after his kidnap, where he was kept as a slave for six years. This period of servitude did not break Patrick, though. From being an idle, aristocratic British boy he progressed, during these years of captivity, into a thoughtful young man who slowly began to see that an important commission was to be placed upon him.

The world Patrick had grown up in was a Britain slowly waking up to the fact that the Roman Empire was never going to return to its shores. For all this, his father was a Romano-British aristocrat who strove to maintain Roman ways. He was a deacon in the Christian Church, and it was from this influence that Patrick would eventually see the path his life was to take. It is also worth mentioning that Patrick's name comes from the Latin *Patricius*, the patrician or noble, a reference to his families' aristocratic background.

Working as a herdsman in what is now Antrim was never going to make Patrick's calling materialise, so he effected his escape and made his way to Brittany. Once there he took advantage of all the resources that were available in a country that had absorbed Christianity deeply. Gaul was at this time still technically a part of the Roman Empire, even if the ties that held it to Rome were ever more strained.

In some respects it might be more useful if the term Empire was never used with regard to Rome. The Romans themselves certainly did not speak of it in anything like the way we refer to it today. Our word Empire is a corruption of their word Imperium, which meant, rather simply, Authority. Rome was the authority that bound a vast military and trading confederation together. Latin was the common language of this confederation, but local customs and speech never went away during the entire 1,000 years that the authority prevailed in the west

In 410 the Emperor Honorius sent a notorious despatch to Britannia telling it to look after its own defences for the time being. The legions did not return, but for a very long time after, Britain continued to regard itself as a part of the Imperium, with or without military support. Across the channel in Gaul the situation was a little more regular, but even there it was clear that control was slipping, and provinces were looking inwards more and more.

Through all the chaos of Rome's decline the Christian Church continued as a centralised organisation that could continue to wield discipline. Patrick was ordained in Brittany, and then spent some time at the Cathedral City of Auxerre, where he studied and broadened his experience. Still a young man, his experiences in Britain, Ireland and Gaul had made him a committed Christian and something of a European, at a time when Europe was beginning its fragmentation into many independent nations.

Patrick's great mission began around 460, but he was being troubled by prophetic dreams for some years prior to this date. At first the dreams simply called him home to Britain but, once there, he was beset by more troubling messages. These implored him to return to Dalriada to preach the word of the Lord. It is impossible to imagine how he must have felt about this summons but, once certain of the calling, he did not hesitate and made the perilous return to the land of his former masters.

Even if Patrick had gone along with his father's view – that the Empire's troubles would eventually pass and everything would return to normal – he was still going out on a limb when he returned to Ireland. This island had never been a part of the Empire and, even as late as the 5th century, the Roman world still regarded it as lying beyond the ends of the earth. They were aware of it, had even briefly considered annexing it, but in the end it remained independent.

Around 460, Patrick made the journey to Irish Dalriada and embarked on a perilous journey to convert the heathen Scots to Christianity. It is not clear if he deliberately chose to emulate St Paul, but he was certainly as committed, and in one respect bolder. He was taking his message outwith the Roman world – something St Paul never considered. This is not to denigrate the activities of Paul, though. Every one of these early evangelists has to be ranked among the bravest souls who have ever walked the earth. Paul was preaching to a hostile and brutally powerful world that was ruled by the mighty Pagan Rome. Patrick was preaching to a defiant and fiercely independent world that had maintained its freedom from Rome, partly through political luck but equally through a ferocious military spirit that the Romans must have been aware of.

The lords of Dalriada were indeed inhospitable to this strange British arrival. Had his years of servitude in Dariada and then the further years of study at Auxerre made him humble? It seems not, for in adopting the title Patricius, he was making a statement about his aristocratic credentials. The Scots were close enough to Britain to be familiar with Latin. He offended many leaders and was imprisoned several times, but he persisted and it may have been his mixture of piety and regal bearing that spared him from summary execution at these times.

One area where he succeeded in at least having his message heard was in his use of existing pagan holy places. If Patrick was to appeal to the religious impulse in the Scots, he was going to have to do it at their religious places. The Christian Church today would regard such an approach as abominable, but it was a policy followed successfully by both the Celtic and Roman Churches for centuries. In this the Pagan world had actually taught the Church; Rome, when it found a native religious centre, would tend to bring up the nearest of its own deities and substitute this for or amalgamate it with the native God. So at Bath we find the British deity, Sulis, being identified with and made one with the Roman deity, Minerva, to give the Roman city a patron deity called Sulis Minerva.

In another area Patrick was also successful. Prior to his arrival in Dalriada, the Pope had despatched one of his own Bishops, Palladius, to convert the whole of Ireland. Palladius was singularly unsuccessful and it was one of the reasons for his failure that improved Patrick's position with the Scots Kings. Rome was then, as now, a centralised hierarchy of priests and bishops. Such a structure was never likely to impress any of the Irish Kings, inside or outside Dalriada. They had a system like the Picts that included the idea of a High King of all Ireland, but in general they worried about their own pride and their own kingdoms. At the time of Patrick's arrival (and presumably Palladius' departure) there were in the region of 150 Irish Kings, all passionately independent and all claiming descent from ancient gods.

Patrick quickly realised that if he promoted the idea of monasticism, he would provide the Scots Kings with an attractive religious system that might entice them from their old beliefs. The idea of separate and independent monastic retreats fitted well with Dalriadan society, which was founded on small clan loyalties. It also flew in the face of Roman Episcopal obedience. If Patrick could establish the Christian faith in Ireland, he might just be able to do so without interference from Rome.

Patrick tirelessly set about his mission, and by the time of his death he had succeeded, so we are told, in making not only Dalriada, but the whole of Ireland, Christian. Whether or not this initial evangelical adventure was the complete success we are led to believe is less important than the fact that the Church Patrick founded was indeed quite independent of Rome and remained so for several centuries. The separate monastic settlements indeed proved popular with the Irish, but there was always the potential for rivalry and hostility between these communities. In 718 the great monasteries of Clonmacnois and Durrow actually went to war with one another, resulting in the deaths of 200 monks.

After Patrick came other brave and aggressive evangelists who, in time, took their message across the North Channel to Alban Dalriada. We have already looked at the life of St Cathan.

In south Kintyre St Kieran is still remembered, as is St Blane, the nephew of St Cathan. There were many others, and by the time of St Columba Alban Dalriada had been Christianised. We must now return to 574, and Columba's choosing and anointing of King Aedan MacGabrain.

While St Columba set out on his great mission to consolidate the Christian faith in Alban Dalriada, and to extend it into the Pagan Pictland, King Aedan was involved in political happenings of the most profound nature. It has been persuasively suggested that Fergus the Great's decision to take his people across the North Channel to Kintyre in 498 was based on an insoluble dispute between the rulers of Irish Dalriada. This said, the links between the two kingdoms remained close, and it was inevitable that, at some point, dispute had to break out over which side of the Channel held the higher status.

This possibility plainly worried the High King of Ireland, Aed, who called a meeting in the second year of King Aedan's rule. The issue at stake was the status of the Dalriadan Scots in Ireland, and it is likely that St Columba was a key player in the final decision. This was a compromise; King Aedan would rule over all Dalriadan Scots, whether in Britain or Ireland. He would levy taxes but he could not call upon them for military support. All military tribute belonged to the High King of Ireland. This was a sensible approach for it reaffirmed the position of the Irish High King. In effect, King Aedan, across the water in Albany, was still a subject ruler under the Irish High Kingship.

What the final decision did not do was please the King of Ulster, who regarded the Irish Dalriadan territories as falling under his rule. The evidence for out and out war between Ulster and Dalriada is scant, but it is plain that Aedan was quite happy to fight with his neighbours where he felt that his interests were being compromised. He is recorded as having battled with the Picts on several occasions, and even took his army against the British. The weakening in stature of the Britons has to be regarded as one of the reasons they eventually fell under Bernician and then Northumbrian rule for so long.

In 603 Aedan fought an inconclusive battle against the Bernicians in Lothian. His activities from this point until his death in 608 are not clear but he seems to have abdicated in favour of his son, Eochaid. What is certain is that, when he died, it was at a monastery at Kilkerran (a district in modern Campbeltown) to which he had retired. This withdrawal to a religious establishment seems to be the source of a story that Aedan was actually ordained as a priest by St Columba. The retreat, coupled with his selection by St Columba, would appear to be the source of this confusion.

Priest, King or both, Aedan was a formidable leader in both Britain and Ireland for a time. His reign saw the extension of the Christian faith into Pictland; he established Alban Dalriada as the pre-eminent Kingdom of the Scots; he may even have married a Pictish princess and become the father of a future Pictish King, thus initiating the inter-mixing of Pictish and Scots blood that would eventually ease Kenneth MacAlpine's route to power over both Kingdoms. His rule was significant for the future of Dalriada, Albany and then Scotland.

The Britannia of St Patrick may have been a Christian land, but by the turn of the 7th century the lands south of Hadrian's Wall had reverted to Paganism. This was mainly down to the now established power of the Anglo-Saxons who had brought their Pagan culture across the North Sea, and had slowly but surely supplanted the native British and Christian culture. Their eventual supremacy continues to this day, but the days of Paganism were numbered.

Sometime after 635 King Oswald of Northumbria sent messengers to the community at Iona, asking that St Aedan be sent to preach to Oswald's largely Pagan people. An impression is often given of the English Kingdoms as completely Pagan, and viciously opposed to the Christian religion. It is certainly true that Christianity had all but disappeared as an established and ordered faith in these countries, but it did still exist. If we go back some 20 years to the time of King Edwin of Northumbria, we find him negotiating to marry the daughter of the King of Kent. This Royal house was Christian, and made it a condition of the match that the entire Kingdom of Northumbria had to be converted to the faith. To this end Paulinus was brought north to begin the task and, with the approval of the Pope, York was elevated to an archbishopric and also Edwin's capital.

By the time of Oswald, Northumbria had again been torn into its original parts of Lothian, Bernicia and Deira. In fact it had not survived Edwin, who was killed in battle in 633. Oswald came to power some time after 635, and, from a power base in Lothian and supported by a Dalriadan army he re-took and re-united Northumbria. The support he received from the Scots deserves to be explained in some detail because it led, not only to the restoration of Northumbria but also to the introduction of Celtic Christianity into this realm.

Edwin had killed Oswald's father, Athelfrith. This led to Oswald and one of his brothers fleeing to Alban Dalriada, a move that demonstrates their desperation as Athelfrith had been an enemy of the Scots King Aedan some years before. It may have been that they had no other recourse than to throw themselves upon someone's mercy, and it seemed likelier that they would receive it in the soundly Christian Dalriada than anywhere else in Britain. As it was, the Scots welcomed the exiles and placed them in the care of the community at Iona, where they were baptised.

The reigning Dalriadan King was Eochaid and, during an exile of more than a decade, young Oswald fought alongside him throughout his campaigns in Ireland. The experience he gained during these conflicts proved invaluable when, in 633, he entered Lothian with his Scots army and proceeded to reclaim his father's Kingdom. The Venerable Bede recorded that Oswald prayed before a decisive battle near Hexham and planted a cross in the battlefield. It is certain that such an act would be unusual for an English warrior of the time, but Oswald was at the head of a Scots Christian army.

Having reunited Northumbria within a few short years Oswald set about introducing the Scots Church to his people. He brought St Aedan from Iona and granted him the island of Lindisfarne, off the Bernician coast in a position not far south of the modern Scottish/English border. Here St Aedan established a community along the model of Iona, and Lindisfarne is alternatively known as Holy Island to this day.

Bringing the Celtic Church to an English Kingdom was a display of Oswald's devotion to the country that had protected him. Although the Celtic tradition was soundly orthodox Christianity, it had practices that made it very distinct from the Roman model and these would have been very obvious to any converts that Paulinus had made during his time at York. As it was, the Roman party had fled after the death of Edwin leaving the field clear for Aedan's people.

Another feature of how adventurous Oswald's intentions were is that Aedan could not speak a word of Anglo-Saxon, and must have appeared extremely alien to the Northumbrians. Oswald, who spoke Gaelic, translated for Aedan and the appearances of these two great leaders, spiritual and temporal, together and united, must have helped in the final conversion of the Northumbrians.

In the south, and to his great credit, Paulinus continued to preach, becoming the first Bishop of Rochester. At first sight this appears potentially contentious – Roman and Celtic Churches divided by national frontiers. In truth all parties saw their role as the conversion of the Pagans. They might not have fully trusted one another, but they must have taken solace from the fact that Christianity was now being aggressively promoted throughout Britain. Indeed, it was with the establishment of the Iona community that the Christianising of all of the British peoples can be said to have begun.

Oswald's rule lasted, surprisingly, for only six or seven years. To have achieved what he did in so short a time is remarkable, and his memory was eventually venerated by his being regarded as a Saint. His end, though, was horrifying. Captured in battle in 642, he was tortured to death in a brutal Pagan killing ritual and his corpse hacked to pieces. It seems perversely appropriate that this King, who did so much to promote the spread of Christianity should have fallen into the hands of the godless at the end.

In 664 Oswald's successor, Oswy, called a Synod at Whitby to debate the issue of the precise dating of Easter. On the surface the reason for Oswy calling the Synod was because he and his wife belonged to different churches; he had been baptised into the Celtic Church, while his wife, Enfleda, belonged to the Roman. While both were orthodox, each used a different method of calculating the date of Easter, the most important festival in any Christian calendar. The gap between the dates was so large that it was possible for Oswy to celebrate Easter while his wife was still fasting through Lent.

Domestic discord was not the only pressure on Oswy. Within his Kingdom, his own son, Alfrith, sub-King of Deira, had embraced the Roman party and had gone as far as expelling Celtic churchmen from the monastery at Ripon. The Synod was an attempt to resolve this growing problem and in the end Oswy found in favour of the Roman party. We will never fully know what moved him in the direction he took. He plainly had a problem with subjects, not least his own son, favouring Rome. Rome was certainly a more powerful ally than the northern Kingdoms of the Scots and Picts, and we have already seen that the Kings of Britain had stronger contacts with Europe than the term 'Dark Ages' would suggest.

The clear advantage to Oswy in supporting the Roman Church had to be balanced against the power base that he held. From 655 onwards he was effectively the Overlord of the English people as he ruled Northumbria and Mercia. His nephew was King of Pictland and he was closely allied with Wessex and Kent. This was a mighty British lord whose authority extended across vast areas of Britain. However, he was still essentially the King of Northumbria and traditionally the focus of his attention would be to the north. Oswy turned against convention and, in doing so, began the process of the English Kingdoms looking to one another and away from Pictland and Dalriada.

Pope Gregory the Great is recorded as the great converter of the Anglo-Saxon peoples. It was he who had sent St Augustine to convert the Jutes of Kent at the end of the 6th century. Certainly the Roman Church was to be the great power of coming centuries, but the great sweep of the Celtic Church out of Ireland, north through Alban Dalriada, into Pictland and then south into Northumbria has to be recognised for the magnificent achievement it was. If the Roman Church brought its influence to bear among the northern English, its task was made all the easier by many of its converts already being Christian.

That Iona is not better regarded in the ecclesiastical history of the English is probably the result of Roman policy rather than English. As we have seen, Northumbria always regarded the north as a legitimate sphere of influence, but after the ascendancy of the Roman Church many things changed in Britain. It is almost a tradition in modern Scotland to see an age-old conspiracy in the vague and unmindful attitude of the English to their northern neighbour, but the fault may be traced more convincingly to events at Whitby in 664. But even this is not the full tale.

It should not be forgotten that, although the English Kingdoms progressively turned their eyes southwards, the northern Kingdoms – particularly after the arrival of the Vikings – were compelled to look to the north and west. Both peoples turned away from one another, but not entirely because of feelings of antipathy. As with all nations and peoples throughout history, forces outwith and beyond their frontiers and control demanded their attentions.

The ascendancy and growth of the Celtic Church lasted a little more than a century before it met Rome head-on in England. It is hard to judge what Columcille (St Columba's true name) would have made of the eventual turn of events, but to close this chapter it may be useful to look at the man behind the priest.

Columba came from the mighty O'Neill clan of Antrim. This family is still represented in Ireland and Argyll; the McNeills were once a very prominent family on Gigha where their descendants still live.

Columba, as well as being a priest, was also a powerful prince of the O'Neills. This worldly background made Columba very different from many of the Saints who would follow him. When Iona was granted to him he never regarded it as a place of seclusion and contemplation. The community was to be a school, and those who would not come for education might only expect Columba and his brothers to come to them. As a prince himself Columba had a clear advantage when it came to the conversion of the Picts. He went right to the top and relentlessly pursued King Brude, eventually convincing him to adopt the new faith.

The conversion of all of Pictland to Christianity was by no means easy, even after Columba's success with Brude. Through his long life he never ceased to move from place to place, attended by his disciples, preaching to the people and setting up monasteries at important locations. By the time of his death in 597 all of what would one day be Albany was Christian. A century later all of Britain was Christian.

Columba was a remarkable man who well deserves the title of *Saint* that was prefixed to his name. His devotion to his cause provokes not only admiration, but also astonishment. At a time when the clergy were not required to be celibate, he and his disciples gave up the distractions of the world and single-mindedly pursued their aims from Iona. The religious structure that they established was also quite different from that of Rome. The many monasteries and cells they established remained for a long time subject to the Abbey at Iona. It has been suggested that this was the source of the Presbyterian system of Church government in Scotland, which is quite distinct from the hierarchical system of the Roman Church.

Ultimately we have to see Columba as a very modern and unsuperstitious individual; 34 years among the Pagan Picts is evidence enough of his dedication. His flight from Ireland to escape a clan feud is evidence enough that he was in no way naïve about the realities of the world. The monastic system that he developed and encouraged was taken straight from St Patrick and reflected the political realities of life in Ireland, Dalriada and Pictand. This was a pragmatist who saw that the world was as much a part of God's realm as any afterlife.

So how would St Columba have reacted to the ascendancy of Rome? Probably with the same pragmatism that he approached everything else. Columba was a Christian and would have rejoiced at the success of any Christian community. The differences between his structures and those of Rome had been largely dictated by the clan systems of the Scots and Picts. If Columba had continued south and into the English Kingdoms he would doubtless have modified the ways in which he planted Christianity to suit local traditions. His mission eventually extended south, as far as Lindisfarne, just as the Roman mission was extending north to meet it.

It is often commented on in the modern era that the Christian world is profoundly divided. Ulster remains a hotbed of religious hatred, which is ironic considering that it was from this very place that Christianity set out into Albany to convert the peoples of Britain. It is doubtful that Columba would have understood the divisions that exist today, for from his perspective and from any rational religious outlook, the differences between the Christian communities in the west are negligible.

No matter what the Church; Roman, Presbyterian, Lutheran, Anglican – all subscribe to the same basic doctrines. The differences rest in the way they are governed, which tends to suggest that the true differences between purportedly Christian communities are ones of history, culture and politics.

For all the alleged differences between the many churches in the world, all genuinely religious people still speak of there being only one true Church. Even in the rigidly anti-Roman Church of Scotland the congregations still refer to themselves as belonging to the 'Holy Apostolic and Catholic Church'. In the east the Greek Orthodox Church takes a different view as to the nature of the Lord from their western counterparts, but beyond this the differences are, again, ones of government rather than creed.

St Columba would doubtless have regarded all of these tricky arguments as no more than an irritation. His task was to extend the Word of the Lord, not to quibble about whether monasticism had more merit than Episcopal discipline. Every soul converted was another notch on Columba's measure of success. Rather than consider how much of a success his mission was it might be better to consider the consequences had he never set out into Pictland.

The Roman party had established itself in Kent before the year 600, but after this there appears to have been very little continuing momentum. It was the advent of Columban priests in Northumbria, effectively ousting the young Roman mission that galvanised activity in the south. It is quite possible that without this northern influence, the Columban Church might have found itself solidly established in the north of Britain with the Roman Church in the south.

There is no question that the Pagan lands between these two Christian powers would eventually have been drawn to one side or the other, but it would certainly have been a considerably slower proposition than what actually transpired. Without Columba the Christianising of Britain would have been a much slower and longer process.

Campbeltown

The seat of the Dukes of Argyll is at Inveraray, but it is 90 kilometres to the south that the town bearing the Campbell name sits. A community has existed at this location for many centuries, but the modern name is first encountered in 1609 when it is used in two charters granting land and detailing the relevant feu duties that were to be paid. Two things are unusual about the use of the name at this time. The first is that *Campbeltoune* existed only as a planned new town in 1609, and the second is that the Earl of Argyle made the choice of name. Naming a town after a family is often done by the natives in honour of that family, but here the Earl was making a point and staking a claim in lands that were traditionally MacDonald, not Campbell. Campbeltown would be the official name of the town from 1609 onwards but for another 70 years the old name, Ceannloch-Kilkerran would be used more often.

Ceannloch-Kilkerran translates quite simply as the Head of Loch Kilkerran. The Kilkerran element was originally Cille Kieran or the Cell of Kieran hence the *Head of the Loch of the Cell of Kieran.* St Kieran is mentioned in the chapter on Gigha as travelling with St Cathan into Alban Dalriada in the early 6th century. He established a church at what is now called Kilkerran, in the south of Campbeltown, but there had been a settlement there since at least the 3rd century, and probably considerably earlier. The deep loch protected by Davaar Island and the sandbar of the Doirlinn is a natural harbour and it is probable that its potential has been exploited for as long as people have lived in Kintyre.

The modern town extends around the north-western end of the loch, but until the 17th century it centred around Kilkerran, almost two kilometres to the south. The town's cemetery, still called Kilkerran, is at the southern end of this area, and parts of this date back to the early 7th century. King Aedan MacGabhran was buried here in April 608, as were other Dalriadan Kings before Iona became an important royal centre. It is today one of the oldest Christian burial sites still in regular use.

The antiquity of the Kilkerran location and a linguistic similarity has created an often repeated but undoubtedly false importance for ancient Campbeltown. The presence of the cemetery, which occupies, at its heart, the site of Kieran's original church, is a permanent reminder of this Patron Saint of Kintyre. There is no doubt that it was an important site but the suggestion that it was once the capital of Dalriada has to be taken with a pinch of salt.

An ancient reference to the area around Campbeltown uses the name Dalruaidh or Ruaidh's Holding. The closeness of this to the word Dalriada has led to the recurring suggestion that the two place names are in fact the same. In one way this is understandable; the variety of spellings of Gaelic words, ancient and modern, is bewildering. In preparing this book I had to often consciously choose a variant and then attempt to maintain it despite finding all manner of spellings in different texts. Even modern resources have failed to find any agreement on these spellings. From the place names Dalruaidh and Dalriada then has come the theory that the Scots Kingdom laid its roots around the Campbeltown area, and then spread north taking the name as it went. While it is agreeable to imagine the town as having an ancient and Royal past the facts simply do not support the theory. Beyond any other argument is the fact that the Scots brought the name Dalriada from their homeland in Ireland. The prefix Dal is also extremely common so using it to support a theory based on a similarity of names is, at best, naïve and, at worst, mischievous. Even the burial of Dalriadan Kings at Kilkerran offers no support for the theory. Iona holds more Royal burials but no one has ever suggested that *it* was the capital of Dalriada.

The building of a castle at Kilkerran in 1490 by King James IV supports the importance of that site. In 1498 charters were issued there *'at the new castle in Kintyre'* so it seems that this structure was not built on a pre-existing site. Some remains are still visible close to the edge of the loch. This structure appears to have been built as a follow up to the forfeiture of the lands of John MacDonald, last Lord of the Isles. That a show of strength was vital is evidenced by this forfeited Lord of the Isles hanging the Governor of Dunaverty Castle in the sight of the King in 1494.

On a nearby hill at Knockbay, Commissioners of King James VI met in 1596 and 1605. Their role was to scrutinise and, if necessary, adjust the titles of all holders of land in Kintyre. The names of these land holders were recorded and show that, in the main, they represented families with an ancient stake in the area before the influx of Lowlanders during the 17th century: McKay, McNeill, McEachran, McShannon and O'May are listed and these names are still to be found in and around Campbeltown – a fact which makes a mockery of suggestions that all MacDonalds and subject clans had been exterminated or ejected from Kintyre by 1599.

The 'Plantation' of Kintyre by Lowlanders and Campbells is difficult to date accurately, but it was certainly inaugurated in the 17th century. By 1678, though, the new immigrants remained centred around Campbeltown and Southend, which should not come as any great surprise. The natives of Kintyre were still coming to terms with the new order of the Campbell Earls of Argyle. Their ancient independence had been protected by the Lords of the Isles but they were now long gone. On top of this sense of a lost culture they were now finding growing numbers of foreigners arriving in their lands. If this description seems extreme it should be remembered that the native people of Kintyre spoke Gaelic, while the Lowlanders spoke Scots or English, both languages kin to one another but completely alien to the Gaels.

It is an often forgotten fact that the plantation of Kintyre with Lowlanders was only one of three similar social and political adventures. The intention in all three cases was to place large lowland populations among the 'wild Irish' of the Highlands and Islands. These populations would then exert control and influence over their Gaelic neighbours, bringing southern civilisation to the wilder extremities of the King's dominions.

It was also hoped that the Gaelic language might be allowed to dwindle in the face of English and Scots, which had the support of the British Crown. There is no evidence that, in these early years, there was any deliberate policy to ban Gaelic and it continued to be the language of the original inhabitants who, for the most part, did not mix or inter-marry with their lowland neighbours. It has, however, been noticed that lowland families who moved north from the Southend and Campbeltown areas, did actually take on Gaelic. This was undoubtedly necessary, as it would have left them as virtual outcasts surrounded by Gaels.

A plantation had been attempted on the Island of Lewis, but the ferocious resistance of the natives had swiftly made this unworkable. With the benefit of hindsight it does seem bold to have made such an attempt at the furthest fringes of the control of the Scottish government. The division of the Scots peoples into Lowland and Highland was well under way at this time, with the Highlanders regarded as a lower form of Scotsman. For the Islanders, though, was reserved a contempt that made them, in the eyes of Lowlanders, little better than animals. On Lewis this nation of sub-humans threw out the incomers.

It was in 1598 that an Act of Parliament was passed to establish three Royal Burghs; in Kintyre, on Lewis and in Lochaber. The overall state of Scotland, though, did not permit these plans to be fully effected at the time of the Act. In fact the only location to receive its burgh was Kintyre at Campbeltown, although it seems that Fort William and Stornoway were eventually developed from the original idea behind the act, even if they never became Royal centres.

In Lewis the King and his advisers granted the lands of the MacLeods to a company of adventurers whose plan was to colonise the territory with lowlanders and then make improvements according to plans suggested. It has to be said that at no time was it the King's intention just to spread civilisation to the areas of the proposed burghs. He had an eye firmly on the improved revenues that would flow from properly controlled and taxed parts of his Kingdom. The great scandal of it all is that it was purely down to King James himself and his extravagant favourites that the state purse was in such a depleted state.

Many factors undid the Lewis adventure, but the least obvious was the secretive efforts of other northern chiefs to place intractable obstacles in its path. If this seems strange we should not forget that these chiefs would have been obviously concerned about their own territories being similarly confiscated and packaged out to other lowland companies.

It was not until October 1599 that the lowland adventurers set out for Lewis. We will never know why they left it so late in the year, but no Scotsman could have been in any doubt about the weather prospects as winter approached. As they should have expected many of the 600 or more who had set out quickly succumbed to illness and died. The weather was freezing, they appear not to have carried adequate provisions, and it proved difficult to establish proper shelters.

Ruari MacLeod was the last undisputed Lord of Lewis, but it was his son, Neill along with brother Murdoch, who subjected the colonists' fledgeling township to repeated raids in 1600. It was lucky for the colonists that these two brothers soon quarrelled. Neill took the side of the colonists against Murdoch, who was eventually taken to Edinburgh and executed. At the same time Neill was pardoned for his activities, and he and the colonists returned to Lewis – both parties feeling more secure for the moment.

It was not to last. By 1601 Neill had quarrelled with one of the colonists' leaders, and blood had been shed. Mackenzie of Kintail – who had been holding Neill's legitimate brother, Tormod, prisoner – immediately, released his captive and sent him to Lewis with a promise of secret assistance. It was more important to Mackenzie that the Lewis colony should be extinguished, rather than he retain his prisoner. Tormod was immediately accepted as Lord and Master of Lewis by his own clan and other natives of the island. With Neill as lieutenant and adviser, the colony was attacked and convincingly defeated. Tormod accepted the surrender of the colony but only under certain conditions, one of which was that they would never return to Lewis.

They immediately planned to return to Lewis with sufficient force to replant their colony, but events in Scotland, not least the King's inheritance of the English throne, delayed matters for several years. In 1605 they finally came back, armed not only with weapons but also with various Crown commissions and powers. For a time they were successful, although Tormod was sent to London where he very nearly convinced the King of the injustice of the plantation.

Neill and his supporters continued to resist the colonists who, by 1607 were thoroughly disillusioned with the whole enterprise. Since the inception of the adventure many had withdrawn; some had died; others had been practically reduced to destitution, while the remainder found that their other business interests were being neglected by the inordinate amount of time and effort they were expending in Lewis. The colony was dismantled and the colonists returned home.

Another plantation was initiated in Ulster after Hugh O'Neill, Earl of Tyrone, and Rory O'Donnell, Earl of Tyrconnel, fled to Rome in 1607. King James VI had their vast estates forfeited to the Crown, and it was to these lands that Protestant settlers would be sent to quench the power of the Catholic natives. By 1640 almost 100,000 British immigrants were planted in Ulster.

To that date within Europe, there had never been so large a movement of people for a political end. But huge as this movement was, it had an ironically unexpected failing built into it. It simply was not huge enough. As events have tragically turned out the planted population never achieved any long-term influence over the native people. A siege mentality quickly set in, and the troubles that still exist in Ulster are a lamentable memorial to the half-realised ambitions of the first King of Great Britain.

There is little point in dwelling on the very obvious failure of the Ulster plantation. That of Lewis is less well known and deserves, at least, to be remembered. It would be easy to question why the plantation policy was not withdrawn after the Lewis failure. It had, after all, proven to be nearly impossible to establish the kind of influence imagined by the policy's architects. The plantation of Ulster, initially under the English Queen Elizabeth, was still in its early days. But the full horror of this ill-conceived social experiment would not be fully played out for centuries.

The third plantation was in Kintyre, which in its earliest stages centred around Campbeltown – earmarked to become a Royal Burgh. The logic in this is plain, and mirrors events in Ulster. The new arrivals were completely foreign to the natives. They spoke a different language and practiced a different faith. The more open minded might have regarded the Highlanders as brother Scots, but in truth any such links were contrived matters of law. These were two alien and foreign cultures thrown together by powerful political figures.

The ascent of the Campbells in Kintyre was confirmed by law a good number of years before it was accepted by anyone in Kintyre. This explains the Earl's decision to rename Kinloch as Campbeltown, and to use the modernised town that he would develop as a base for the immigration of people who would support his rule and, if required, supply troops to fight on his behalf.

It was long assumed that the Earl of Argyle brought his Lowlanders into Kintyre with all manner of inducements, but appears not to have been the case. The new arrivals entered into contracts with the Earl and paid the going rate for the lands they took charge of. This seems to support the entire reasoning behind inviting these people in the first place. They were regarded as honest, thrifty and hard working: attributes that were unlikely to be drawn to short-term incentives.

There is much dubiety about events following the plantation, but a couple of things differentiate Kintyre from its two counterparts. In the first place there was no large resistance by the natives, as in Lewis. The two communities quite quickly settled down to a distant co-existence. It was recorded as late as the 19th century that the Highlanders and Lowlanders still had very little to do with one another, and inter-marriage was unheard of. In the second place there was no development of opposed and entrenched communities, as in Ulster. This might seem an odd comment given the lack of communication between the communities but there is an enormous difference between peoples who have little to do with one another and peoples who are hell-bent on the destruction of one another.

It is difficult to understand why the Kintyre plantation prospered. Perhaps because it was a mainland territory of the Crown, not separated by difficult waters from the King's power base, was one reason. Or maybe the fact that the new arrivals took possession of their lands as businessmen rather than conquerors helped. This, however, had not helped their counterparts on Lewis. But prosper it did, in spite of the turbulent century that witnessed its beginnings.

One thing that quickly differentiated it from Lewis was that it spread from original bases. The spread was hardly meteoric, but there was never the stockade and siege mentality that had marked the Lewis colony and would, in time, become a feature of Protestant landholders in Ulster surrounded by Roman Catholic natives.

However, it should be pointed out that while there was little direct hostility to the Lowlanders, the natives were seldom disposed to making any show of welcome. The Lowland Church in Campbeltown was founded in 1654 to answer the need of its parishioners, who had no place of worship of their own; the existing churches all conducted services in Gaelic. It has also been suggested that the situation was so difficult in the early years that some settlers would return to their home parishes across the Firth of Clyde for communion, marriage and baptism.

The issue of Highland and Lowland congregations was never fully resolved. In 1806 a new Highland Church was opened, but only after the congregation had been compelled to use the Lowland Church on Castlehill for more than 20 years, after their own building had fallen into ruin. To this day in Campbeltown there are still a Highland and a Lowland Church; both Church of

Scotland, both conducting services in English, but both coming from different heritages. It is pleasing, though, to record that the animosity between the congregations is now a thing of the distant past.

Campbeltown finally became a Royal Burgh in 1700, the only one of the three planned a century before. By this time it was clear that the plantation had been a success. I would argue that a measure of this success is the modern attitude of the native population, who see no distinctions among themselves. The terms 'incomer' or 'stranger' are reserved for recent arrivals from other parts of Scotland. For anyone whose family has resided in the town into a second (some argue a third) generation is reserved the title of native. No thought is given to the ancient Lowland and Highland distinctions and even the odd inter-marriage has been recorded.

From the founding of the Burgh the history of Campbeltown and Argyll fall more closely into the broader picture of Scotland. With the Campbell Dukes of Argyll now undisputed lords of what was once Dalriada, the ancient sense of separateness receded somewhat. As has been recorded the Dukes of Argyll generally, though by no means always, supported the Government position, whether that was the Scottish or British Government. From being a remote, foreign and potentially hostile place, Argyll became firmly bound up with the destiny of Scotland.

When suggesting once that Campbeltown might do well to emulate Oban, in the north of Argyll, and become a tourist centre, I was rather indignantly informed that the Royal Burgh was "a market town." I have to concede that my precise remark involved suggesting that an amusement arcade be built close to the waterfront, but the response was remarkable in that it took little account of two things. The first was the unavoidable necessities of economics and the second was the history of Campbeltown itself. At no point has this remarkable little town, affectionately referred to as 'The Wee Toon', ever been exclusively given up to one commercial pursuit.

Surrounded by farms, there is no doubt that Campbeltown does deserve a reputation as a market town. However, in the 21st century, the need to distribute goods through the nearest sizeable urban outlet no longer exists. Our elaborate transport system means that more and more produce is transported directly to processors and distributors. An annual agricultural show does, however, continue to take place every August, as an ongoing reminder of Kintyre's farming roots. It is to be hoped that this will always be the case, but invariably it is with more than a little sadness that I contemplate a grand selection of photographs on the walls of Gigha Hotel's homely little bar, which portray the island's annual agricultural highlight, now long since abandoned. Ultimately it is the market in its larger sense that will determine the focus of a community's enterprise.

A famous music hall song happily wishes that Campbeltown Loch consisted entirely of whisky. A story told in the town is that *'Campbeltown Loch, I wish it were whisky'* is based on a real event when fires in distilleries along Glebe Street released thousands of litres of whisky which poured down the towns gutters and into the loch. The extent of the outflow was evidence enough of how vast the Campbeltown whisky industry formerly was. An alternative explanation of the song is that it simply records the massive output from these distilleries. Between 1880 and 1920 there were 34 working distilleries producing more than 9,000,000 litres of whisky a year. For a time, Campbeltown was running neck and neck with Elgin as the whisky capital of Scotland.

From the 18th century Campbeltown was also a coal centre. Coal had been mined on a small scale from the 15th century, but by the late 1700s the industry was large enough to require the building of a canal from Machrihanish to Campbeltown to make transportation easier. A century later a railway line was built to speed up this transport.

Period photographs show the town's Old Quay filled with barrels of herring that had just been put ashore for salting. The extent of the catches is breathtaking; there is hardly a square centimetre of the extensive quay not covered in barrels, and here we have another vanished Campbeltown industry. The factor that sent the fishing into a downward spiral was ecological rather than commercial. The shoals of herring became much more sporadic and the ring-net method, as a large-scale enterprise, eventually petered out completely in the late 1960s. A greatly reduced fleet of small inshore trawlers and creel boats employing only around 25 men now concentrates on prawn and crab fishing.

RAF Machrihanish was for some years a base for American forces, a presence that brought considerable financial benefits to Campbeltown. As with most such stations in Europe, the Americans departed in the 1990s. In general when this occurred the British Government compensated the communities that were losing the American presence. In the case of Campbeltown, though, it was decreed that Machrihanish had never been a formal US base, rather an RAF base leased to the Americans. Following their departure, the Ministry of Defence decided to maintain the base as an active RAF location, officially designated as *under enhanced care and maintenance status*. The upshot of this was that Campbeltown, unlike towns such as Dunoon, got no compensation since RAF Machrihanish continued to be an active British base. The fact that there are no military personnel stationed there has left a sour taste in the mouths of most locals. Unfortunately, this is not the only instance where Campbeltown has been overlooked for resourcing that has subsequently gone to other towns, mainly to other parts of Argyll.

It is a significant fact, and proof that the town has a broader importance than simply agriculture, that in 1900 Campbeltown had the highest per capita income in Scotland. A legacy of this is the large number of beautifully constructed properties, not only in the more upmarket Askomil area, but also in the solidly built tenement buildings along Longrow. There is also a wonderful library that held a substantial collection of works until this was, controversially, broken up and sent to Edinburgh.

Campbeltown's fortunes during the 20th century varied, but it is a well-known fact that this period saw the decline of many traditional industries. Among these were coal, fishing and agriculture – all closely bound up with Campbeltown. It was also at this time that Argyll again became remote from the rest of Scotland, due to increasing numbers of rural people moving to the cities, leaving the countryside an emptier place. In 1900, a turbine steamer could reach Glasgow from Campbeltown in four to five hours. Incredibly, in 2000 the journey by coach could take the same length of time, depending on weather and traffic delays.

The remoteness from the rest of Scotland has also turned into distance from the rest of Argyll, and the level of neglect by the ruling Argyll and Bute Council became something of a scandal as the 21st century began. Resources that were needed in Campbeltown were, incomprehensibly, diverted to Dunoon, an already wealthier town. This action renewed previous calls for the return of a properly accountable local authority, rather than the representatives who seemingly carried no weight in pressing issues of concern to Kintyre.

Another social concern that transpired during the last decade of the 20th century, and continued into the new century, was the movement of people with drug, alcohol and behavioural problems into Campbeltown – a topic which has devoured many column inches of the local newspaper's readers' letters page. This appears to emanate from agreements between local authorities and cities such as Glasgow. Whatever inducements were made between the relevant administrations is unknown to me, but subsequent developments in Campbeltown have shown that entire areas of public properties have become seriously unattractive to genuine local people or bona fide newcomers to the town. At the time of writing, the Park Square and Parliament Place housing developments have more windows boarded up than curtained. Apparently, plans are afoot to demolish the properties and recreate new housing units. This is a profound shame, since the buildings in question are perfectly adequate and the areas were once pleasant locations to live in and bring up families. This short sighted and socially destructive policy has to be seen as another example of increasingly apparent local authority disregard for the entire Kintyre area.

It is important in this chapter's conclusion to emphasise that Campbeltown still exists in the 21st century, and is still very much a living, healthy community. The above problems are probably no worse than in other Scottish towns; perhaps they are more obvious in a small geographically challenged community, but the town's remoteness from the thoughts and policy of its leaders certainly must be the single biggest issue that needs addressing.

There has been a community at the *Head of the Loch of the Cell of Kieran* for as long as there has been recorded history in Scotland, and probably for longer even than that. The land around it has been called Kintyre, Argyll, Dalriada, Dalruidh, Scotland, Great Britain and doubtless scores of names before history was written down. All the ancient names have passed away, and perhaps so will the current names in time, but it is safe to assume that for as long as there is a head of the loch, there will be a community there, whatever it will be called.

Dunaverty

On July 10, 1647, 300 members of the MacDonald Clan held the castle of Dunaverty against a besieging force. The castle had been a stronghold for centuries prior to this date, and was eminently well suited its role. Dun Abhairtach, to give it its original title, was named after a powerful Irish tribe and occupied a 27-metre tall plug of rock at the south of Kintyre, close to the modern village of Southend. On the seaward side the rock front is steep and unassailable, and a deep chasm extends along the landward side. The rock is a superb defensive position with only one weakness to which we will return.

Historically, Dunaverty's location has been significant. It was the place where Fergus the Great landed with his followers from Irish Dalriada in 498. He brought with him the Stone of Destiny and it was at Dunaverty that this legendary relic first touched the soil that would one day be Scotland. During the rule of the Vikings Dunaverty was their principle stronghold on the mainland, and their main rendezvous point was at Sanda Island, two kilometres out to sea. Robert the Bruce was entertained here for most of the time he was assumed to be hiding on Rathlin Island, off the north coast of Ireland. After the King came to power his brother, Prince Edward, set out from here in 1315 on the ultimately disastrous Scottish campaign in Ireland. The King had hoped to establish a second front in his war against Edward II of England, but his dream of a combined Caledonia and Hibernia, ruled jointly with his brother, collapsed into chaos and disaster. By 1318 Prince Edward was dead, and the remains of the Scots army had returned across the North Channel to Dunaverty.

As the nearest point of communication between Scottish and Irish Dalriada, Dunaverty was for long an important link in communications between the two lands. At a later date, when the ancient links had become less solid, it remained the practice of the MacDonald Lords of the Isles to proclaim newly enacted Laws –

with great ceremony – at Dunaverty, even after it ceased to be the capital, which had eventually moved north to Kinloch (modern Campbeltown).

In 1647, the rock remained a formidable fortification, and the defenders looking out over the landward chasm to the besieging army would have been well aware of this. In command of the MacDonald garrison was Archibald MacGillespick, the brother of the clan chief, Sir Alexander MacDonald. Sir Alexander's father was aged but very much alive at this time, yet he appears to have sensibly deferred to his militarily more experienced son. The old MacDonald's full name was Coll MacGillespick Vic Coll MacDonald but he was better known by the nickname *Coll Kittoch* (alternatively *Coll Kittach*, *Coll Ciatach* or *Collkitto*) that referred, in Gaelic, to his left-handedness. We shall return to Coll Kittoch because he was directly involved in the fortunes of the MacDonalds in the early 1600s which, in due time, had a great bearing on the events of 1647.

MacGillespick's garrison had arrived at Dunaverty on May 26 as part of a larger force. A few hours march to the north, at Kinloch, the forces of General David Leslie and the Marquis of Argyle (*Argyll* is a modern spelling) were resting, having pursued the MacDonalds southwards through Kintyre. By this time Sir Alexander MacDonald had split his force. Leaving a garrison of 300 at Dunaverty, his remaining 500 men sailed to Islay. Once there, old Coll Kittoch was left in command of the castle of Dunaovaig with 200 men while Sir Alexander departed again, this time for Ireland where he hoped to muster more troops from among the MacDonalds of Antrim.

Sir Alexander's plan was to return across the North Channel and relieve the garrison as soon as possible. When rested, his fresh troops would march against General Leslie and the Marquis and retake Kintyre. As it turned out, Sir Alexander was killed in Ireland and no relief ever came to Dunaverty. Local tradition, however, tells that MacDonald *did* return. There are two variations of this story. In the first, a piper playing from the seaward cliff-face warns off MacDonald's vessels; in the second, the MacDonalds actually land but are beaten back by Leslie's troops.

The above local stories highlight a difficulty with the history of this forgotten corner of Scotland. There are often two opposite views of the same events, and the side taken depends on which clan the reader favours most. The return of MacDonald is plainly given little credence by supporters of the Marquis' clan, the Campbells. Indeed an eyewitness to the events at Dunaverty does not mention any landing or attempt at landing. This was Sir James Turner, who was with Leslie's army, but his testimony is reliable enough to be confident that he would have mentioned an engagement, had there been one.

By the time General Leslie and the Marquis of Argyle arrived, along with more than 2,000 troops (including cavalry) Archibald MacGillespick, assisted by his son, Archibald Oig MacDonald had strongly fortified Dunaverty. The impregnable fortress stood ready for a vigorous and prolonged defence.

Superficially we see at this siege a clan feud between the formerly powerful MacDonalds and the aggressive and rising Campbells. There is some truth in this, since Sir Alexander very clearly intended to win back the ancient holdings of his family – Kintyre and Islay. Equally the Marquis of Argyle had no intention of surrendering these territories, which had only come to the Campbells a generation before.

Argyll in its modern form is a vastly larger territory than the original northern heartland and earldom of Argyle. The Campbell Earls of Argyle had, by fair means or foul, successfully extended their control south into Lorne and then into Kintyre, creating the mainland territory that is now Argyll. The modern seat of the Campbells is quite centrally placed at Inveraray, which is some distance from the clan's ancient rallying point at Ben Cruachan. This impressive mountain stands at the northern boundary of modern Argyll and ancient Dalriada. Its significance to the Campbells is plain in their battle cry that is simply *Cruachan!*

As Campbell power grew, it generally did so at the expense of the MacDonalds, who were the successors of the Lords of the Isles. The Campbells were also fortunate in often achieving advancement for their clan, while at the same time promoting the interests of the nation as a whole. Such a path is always tricky, and at times it is difficult to gauge just where the broader interest lies. The year 1647 was just such a time as the British nations were being torn apart by civil war.

Nine years earlier, on February 28, 1638 a 'National Covenant' was signed at Greyfriars Church in Edinburgh. The same day ministers and town leaders signed it, and the following day common people began appending their names. The Covenant essentially claimed to protect the King's peace, but it was also an affirmation of the signatories' determination to maintain the Presbyterian Church in the face of King Charles' equally solid determination to force Episcopal worship down Scotland's throat. The Covenant very quickly became the benchmark by which true Christians and true Scotsmen were measured.

Two years earlier, King Charles had attempted to force an authorised Prayer Book on the Scottish Church, which led to widespread rioting. Charles is a hard person on whom to place convenient descriptions. His bullying actions have all the marks of an uncaring tyrant, but there is much about him that belies this. Perhaps his actions are best explained by his inflexible belief in the Divine appointment of Kings. Placed on his throne by God, Charles had no need to consider the desires and demands of his subjects. It was his duty to rule with strength and benevolence, and God would assist him in this. Guided by Divine providence, the King's will would be obeyed by his subjects who would obtain their happiness and security by their obedience. Unfortunately, in those explosive days, many of the King's Scots and English subjects disagreed violently with this despotic vision.

While many Scots disagreed with the King, many were not for revolution. As 1638 passed, though, the Covenanters, as the Presbyterian party were becoming known, pressed ahead with acts of overt defiance. The General Assembly of the Kirk in

Glasgow severed all connections between the Scottish Church and the English Government. To Charles this meant that his plan to have a single Episcopalian Church throughout Great Britain would now have to be forcibly imposed.

Aware that the King would reply with force, the Covenanters set about building an army to defend Scotland. By the spring of 1639 this force numbered almost 30,000 men. As expected, Charles responded by building a force in England to move north and crush the Covenanters. Fortunately, this force was plainly not sufficient to crush the Scots and the outcome was that battle was avoided and a meeting took place at Berwick-on-Tweed in June 1639.

At this meeting King Charles again exhibited the full arrogance of his Divine Appointment. Seemingly unaware that the Scots were quite capable of crushing his poorly equipped, poorly motivated and poorly led English force, he simply resorted to telling them off. He instructed that the matters at issue should be fully discussed by a Scottish Parliament. The Scots agreed to this and signed a 'Pacification' to this effect.

Charles doubtless regarded this as confirmation of his authority and powers of diplomatic persuasion. It never occurred to this blinkered and poorly advised man that the Scots did not regard themselves as rebels. There were issues that the Covenanters wished to be addressed, but in these early stages they wanted them brought before the King. The thought of taking up arms against Charles was always to be a last resort, but the King never saw this. Though he might not have been the monster some would have us believe, he never took a moment to consider the turmoil that must have been at work within many of the Covenanters. He simply saw rebels in arms against his lawful rule.

It is not the purpose of this book to explore matters such as the Covenant and the Civil War in detail. Suffice to say that in 1644 the Marquis of Montrose took up arms in support of King Charles. The Pacification agreed at Berwick-on-Tweed five years earlier had been used by the King merely to buy time. Incapable of hearing adverse counsel from the start, Charles got no better with the passing years. Indeed, it is unlikely his counsellors ever gave the him the full and balanced information he so desperately needed to hear. The King of Scotland, England and Ireland was presiding over the imminent destruction of all three.

Few would deny that war is always a terrible political outcome, but civil war must surely be the worst of all conflicts. In the Civil War (which was most emphatically a British war, and not simply English) the people were torn between their loyalty to the King and, in Scotland, to the Covenant. James Graham, Marquis of Montrose, made his decision in 1644, and set out to open a second front for the King in the northern and western highlands.

Montrose's force was small but, at this time, it had one great advantage. The bulk of the Covenanter army was stationed in England, and the English Parliament was in no position to release it from its duties there. Montrose's plan then was simple: rally the Highlands and Islands to the Royalist cause, and then move through the sparsely defended lowlands to Edinburgh. Once there, overthrow the Covenant and impose Royalist Government. As success followed success, Montrose could envisage the next step in his plan: when Scotland was securely back in the Royalist camp, he would move south and crush Parliamentary resistance in England as well.

Helping the Marquis cut his swathe of destruction through Scotland was Alexander MacDonald. The son of Coll Kittoch had arrived from Ireland with a force of 2,000, drawn from among his cousins, the MacDonalds of Antrim. MacDonald's landing, at Ardnamurchan, certainly met with the approval of King Charles, but it is not easy to establish whether the King actually instructed it. Such an act, allegedly as part of a 10,000 strong Catholic army, would have been difficult to justify. Even the Divine Right of a King can be stretched to a limit and no further.

It is more likely that MacDonald realised the King's burning desire for troops and also saw, in that need, a chance to restore some of his clan's battered pride. His arrival reached the ears of the Marquis of Argyle, who took immediate action. Whatever MacDonald's asserted aims were, it was Campbell lands that were going to be at the receiving end first. As expected, MacDonald's mixed force of Irish, Highlanders and his Kintyre kinsmen devastated the whole district surrounding their landing point. Campbell, though, acted without hesitation and moved against the invader who sensibly crossed firstly to the Isle of Skye and then back to the mainland at Kintail in Ross-shire.

At a safe distance from the Marquis of Argyle for the time being, Alexander MacDonald set out across Ross, Caithness and Sutherland, presenting himself as an officer of the King. His brutal demands that the inhabitants attend him in this capacity failed and he moved south towards Athol. Here, the Marquis of Montrose whose name and rank as King's Lieutenant General had drawn many of the men of Athol, joined him and the two forces combined into a substantial army. Montrose assumed command as Lieutenant-General and MacDonald was appointed Major-General under him. Joined by others, the Generals of the Royal Army now endeavoured to find and engage the Covenanters.

The progress of the Royal Army became for a time unstoppable, and the banner of King Charles was soon flying over Perth, Angus and Aberdeen. At Aberdeen in particular the conduct of the Royalists was so inhumanly severe that it has been blamed for a sense of mistrust that still exists between the Scots and Irish to this day in some quarters.

During the later stages of Montrose's success, Campbell was again hot on his tail. As he approached Aberdeen the Royal Army quit the city and retreated to the mountains, where it was depleted by desertions. Intent on replenishing his force, Montrose returned to Athol, while, at the same time, he sent Major-General MacDonald back to the Highlands to recruit the clans to the Royal cause.

This might have been an opportunity for Campbell to defeat MacDonald, but his army had been sorely neglected by Parliament. Constantly harrying the Royalists and forcing them to keep moving, his troops had finally given in to hunger, exhaustion and decaying equipment. In the face of an epidemic of desertions, Campbell finally ceded. He made his way to Edinburgh where, with no attempt to conceal his disgust, he resigned his commission.

Montrose and MacDonald now had no enemy in the field. They quickly made their way from Athol to Argyle and Lorne, and mercilessly ravaged the entire area. As the Highland winter took hold, every inhabitant the Royalists encountered was either brutally murdered or thrown out to survive, or otherwise, in the bleakness of the snow. Property was completely destroyed: buildings, furniture, stock, food, and clothing. Anyone familiar with the atrocities of the 20th century would find much that was familiar in the silent landscape of Argyle and Lorne. This was a horrific expedition where the excesses of human barbarity were practiced. Catholic Royalist troops played out their religious and political fervour on their Covenanter enemies and, to this boiling mass of hatred, the MacDonalds added their heart-deep loathing of everyone connected with Clan Campbell. Politics, religion and private revenge turned Argyle and Lorne into a passable representation of Hell on earth.

The Marquis of Argyle may have resigned his commission in the Convenanter army, but it was his own lands that were under the sword. The brutalised corpses lying undecayed on the frozen ground were kinsmen under his protection. With the same resolution that had sent him in pursuit of Alexander MacDonald in the first place, the Marquis raised 3,000 men and went looking for him and his commander Montrose once again.

On February 2, 1645 the armies met at Inverlochy, but this time, flushed with his successes, Montrose did not run. Instead, he ordered an immediate charge that shattered the Marquis' army. As many as 1,500 men were killed in the rout that followed, including many Campbell chiefs. The survivors took to the hills and, in a single blow, the Royalists again had no enemy to face in the field.

After this battle Montrose and MacDonald took full advantage of their position. Moving through Scotland they assumed the role of King's Lieutenant, and ordered all able-bodied men to join the Royal Army. The merest suggestion of hesitation by anyone had him or her instantly treated as a rebel. This involved treatment only slightly less severe than that meted out on the battered inhabitants of Argyle and Lorne. Through 1645 Montrose brought death and destruction throughout the north-east of Scotland. Elgin, Cullen and the seat of the Earl of Findlater were burned to the ground *after* paying Montrose off. Aberdeen successfully avoided another sack by paying the demanded ransom. Stonehaven was not so lucky, and was left a smoking ruin.

While Generals Montrose and MacDonald asserted the King's authority, elsewhere in Argyle and Lorne an old and unwelcome face had reappeared. Coll Kittoch, after the landing at Ardnamurchan (but almost certainly, in a subordinate role), appears to have fought with his son, Alexander. Following the rout at Inverlochy he detached his force, supplied by the Earl of Antrim, and invaded Kintyre. This was exactly to be expected now that the Marquis of Argyle had been defeated. What is remarkable about Coll Kittoch's actions is that he was effectively *commissioned* to perform them by his son, who declared that Kintyre and Islay belonged to him personally.

During his time with the Royal Army, Alexander MacDonald was knighted by Montrose in the name of the King. It was after being knighted that Sir Alexander gave his father the above commission, and it is fair to assume that he regarded himself personally as a legitimate representative of King Charles. That he acted like a King has been suggested, but this is not easy to support. At the time he was still a subordinate of Montrose, and this subordination was reinforced by the fact that it was Montrose who conferred his knighthood. Perhaps the image of a MacDonald clan chief returning to Kintyre and Islay has conjured a latter day comparison with the long departed Kings of the Isles.

Precisely why Sir Alexander was the de facto head of Clan MacDonald while his father still lived is not clear, but Coll Kittoch seems to have been quite content to defer to his son. It may be that Alexander's aspirations were larger than his father's, and there is little doubt that the aged MacDonald was quite satisfied to have his clan's historical lands restored to his control.

The Kintyre he entered was still inhabited, but those who were able to had long since bolted. The large-scale plantation of Lowlanders was some years in the future, but there was a substantial fledgeling settlement particularly in and around Kinloch. These people certainly fled across the Firth of Clyde to Ayrshire, where they joined the Covenanter Army and, in due course, returned.

Coll Kittoch, then, took up residence at the Castle of Kinloch from where he parcelled out Kintyre and Islay amongst his followers. It goes without saying that many families remaining in the invaded lands, not only MacDonalds, took the side of the new Lord. There was no indication that relief would ever arrive and, if terms could be agreed, it was simply a matter of replacing one master with another. For many MacDonalds though, following Coll would have been quite natural. There were many arms of Clan MacDonald but all were ultimately bound together by ancient blood.

A tale told about Coll Kittoch at this time gives an idea of the sort of man he was. Once settled into his new possessions he quickly displayed his ferocious brutality; wanton, random and pointless murder became par for the course. We should not be in the least surprised at this. He and his followers were part of the army that had so recently laid Argyle and Lorne waste. Always armed with a sword, he was also in the habit of carrying a gun which he named *The Gouk*. With this weapon he was in the habit of arbitrarily shooting at anyone he even suspected of dissent. When his victim fell, Coll Kittoch would say drily, "the Gouk has fallen on the poor man." There appears to be no such word in Gaelic but Scots has a similar word 'Gowk'. One of its meanings is 'a look'. He dwelt in Kintyre for three years, and we will never know how many victims fell under Coll Kittock's 'Look'.

At this time Coll Kittoch was in his 70s, and he must have been a remarkable man. At a time when most of his contemporaries would have been dead or infirm he was fighting alongside his son. As a young man in the early days of the reign of James the VI & I he had witnessed the last resistance of his grandfather, Sir James MacDonald, to the Campbells taking control of Kintyre. This MacDonald brought war to Kintyre in his attempt to restore his ancient rights, but ultimately his rebellion was suppressed and he escaped to exile.

In the slow decline of the MacDonalds and the relentless rise of the Campbells to take their place we can see the seeds of a clan rivalry more bitter than any other. In certain ways this is ironic because Sir James MacDonald was married to a Campbell, and his great rival, the Earl of Argyle eventually joined him in exile; the two men were, in their later years, reconciled. Some 30 years later Sir James' successor was an altogether rougher character, and the thought of Coll Kittoch ever entertaining genial thoughts about the Campbells is sadly absurd.

The later successes of the Campbells, in extending the power of their clan, were in some measure mirrored in the political manoeuvres of Sir James MacDonald in the late 16th and early 17th centuries. He was frequently successful in maintaining his position, despite the opposing efforts of the Crown. Here was the big difference between him and his Campbell successors: they succeeded with the actual or tacit support of the King. MacDonald pursued his own aims, with little regard for the person or aims of the King. Such a position was unsustainable in the long term and during the reign of James VI & I MacDonald power was thoroughly crushed.

After Sir James escaped into exile, Coll Kittoch, who was the son of his only daughter, succeeded him. Coll was, from a very young age, a ferocious enemy of the protestant faith. Whether this qualified him as a dutiful Catholic is another question entirely, but his name became quickly known to the Government as a bandit and rebel. His later life, strutting about Kinloch, wielding the infamous 'Gouk' was little different from that of his youth. Murder, brigandage, and all manner of criminality were the day-to-day fare of this vicious young man.

At this time the remoteness of the Highlands and the wildness of its inhabitants meant that the Government had to take a very measured approach to maintaining order there. In general it was left to the local earls and clan chiefs to keep what peace they could. The King's Peace, one suspects, was not a phrase that fell from too many tongues in these places. Fully aware of this, the Government tended to keep its distance so long as the flow of taxes was not disrupted.

Leaving local order to local leaders has its merits, but one thing the Government could not ignore forever was that the inhabitants of the Highlands, as well as being tenants of these local lords, were also subjects of the King. Although low on the priorities of the nation as a whole, the calls for justice from these people had to be addressed at sometime.

In 1614 Coll went too far. The provocation was probably his involvement in a rebellion on Islay, and the Crown was no longer prepared to tolerate his continual defiance. The Government's instrument would be the Earl of Argyle, who was in the process of suppressing a clan insurrection in the north. Finished there, he moved south to fulfil his new commission. Coll though, acted quite unexpectedly. He took to the sea for Ireland, and the protection of his uncle, the Earl of Antrim. Without a shot being fired or a sword drawn, the Earl of Argyle came into possession of Kintyre, which then passed forever from the MacDonalds to the Campbells.

This period is one of some confusion. The Earls of Argyle were now, by Royal decree, the holders of Kintyre and Islay, but it would appear to have been the Royal will for some years prior to this date. The fact that they were unable to make anything of their possessions was down to the fact that the MacDonalds disagreed violently with the Royal will and resisted it wherever they could. Opposition to the Crown was an age-old and passionate pastime of Clan MacDonald, but this throw of the dice would be their last independent clan rising.

The extent of the MacDonald failure was well demonstrated in 1617, when the Earl of Argyle carried the Crown of King James VI at the State Opening of Parliament. In the same year an Act of Ratification confirmed and clarified the position of Kintyre as a Campbell possession. This Ratification went into some detail as to which Campbell heirs held which territories and how rents were to be allocated. In the detailed but mundane legal documents of the period we see that the days of MacDonald greatness had passed away. The Campbells were now the Lords of Argyle, Lorne, Kintyre, Islay and Jura.

But the MacDonalds had not conveniently disappeared with the ascent of the Campbells. Through the 17th century they would be a sporadic thorn in the flesh of both the Scottish Government and Clan Campbell; indeed these two continued often (but not always) to walk parallel courses.

After his flight to Ireland, Coll Kittoch took on the mantle of a career rebel. In 1641 he was arrested by the Marquis of Argyle, but appears to have escaped shortly afterwards, although he may have been released. The politics of the time created strange situations: those in favour could be denounced as rebels a year later. Survivors of rebellions, whose compatriots had been hanged en masse, could find themselves pardoned and pensioned within a few years. Coll Kittoch could be in the hands of the Campbells in 1642 but by 1644 he was the brutal master of Kinloch.

The Royalist cause suffered a crucial setback from the most unlikely of sources in 1646. King Charles surrendered to the Scots Covenanter army at Newark. This was even more devastating than their defeat at Philiphaugh the year before and came as bitter blow to Montrose. The subsequent terms agreed between the King and Parliament led to Charles ordering Montrose to lay down his arms, which he dutifully did. In the west, though, Sir Alexander MacDonald ignored the order and continued to hold out for the Royalist cause. In this we can see some of his true motivation. For a Royal General to ignore the orders of his King suggests that his attachment to the King's cause was led by something other than loyalty. This is further confirmed by his decision to move his troops into Kintyre to join those of his father.

In 1647 the Scottish Parliament was at last able to take the battle to MacDonald. Under Lieutenant-General David Leslie a small army moved into Argyle to face a reportedly smaller force under Sir Alexander. The government force was larger, but there was an ongoing threat that substantial reinforcements might arrive from Antrim.

James Turner (who was later knighted) served as Leslie's adjutant and his is the only eyewitness account we have of the subsequent siege of Dunaverty. Turner's motives in joining Leslie appear strange, as he was a Royalist, but he felt that MacDonald had deserted Montrose before his defeat at Philliphaugh, and wished to be part of the force that would bring some vengeance upon him. The Marquis of Argyle joined Leslie at a later date as commander of a brigade of Highlanders, as did his cousin, Campbell of Ardkinglas, commanding another brigade. To this force were added three troops of cavalry, although some reports suggest Leslie may have had twice this number.

The chaplain of Argyle's brigade deserves some mention here, since his name still has a wicked notoriety attached to it. Reverend John Nave (also Naves, Nevay or Nevoy) will feature strongly in events immediately following the siege. Suffice to say, at this stage, that Reverend Nave was a notably fanatical clergyman at a time when fanaticism was a widespread manifestation of the era.

On May 24, 1647 General Leslie's force entered Kintyre unopposed. In a military sense this is astonishing. The most unmilitaristic person can see, even today, that the passes into the peninsula favour a defender more than an attacker, but Sir Alexander, for reasons we will never know, did not even set observers at these crucial places. Sir James Turner was in no doubt that this was madness, for he states: "Both before and at the entry to it, there were such advantages of ground that our foot, for mountains and marshes, could never have drawn up one hundred in a body, nor our horses above three in a breast, which, if Sir Alaster (Alexander) had prepossessed, with these thousand or twelve hundred brave foot he had with him, I think he might have ruined us, at least we should not have entered Kintire…"

As the sun was setting on May 24, General Leslie engaged the MacDonalds at Rhunahaorine Point and put them to flight. Leslie lost less than 10 men to more than 50 on the MacDonald side. As darkness fell he disengaged and fell back to await the arrival of the main part of his army. MacDonald defences in the north of Kintyre had been so inadequate that Leslie's cavalry had outrun his infantry by over 30 kilometres unopposed.

General Leslie attempted now to secure boats to prevent the departure of the enemy by sea. In this he was unsuccessful and a large number escaped, firstly to Gigha, and then onwards to Islay. The remainder of the army retreated south to Kinloch, from where another large group left by sea. This group was bound for Ireland but first it headed for Islay to pick up Sir Alexander, who had departed from Rhunahaorine the previous day. Sir James Turner's account is difficult to follow here. He suggests that Sir Alexander deployed troops at Dunaverty *before* leaving Kintyre. The difficulty here is whether he ordered the placement or was actually there to oversee it.

Whatever the truth, Sir James Turner is scathing in his regard for Sir Alexander's skills as a general and, indeed, a soldier. There is nothing in historical or modern warfare, though, that suggests a General should stand with his troops to the inevitable and bitter end. For all his protestations, General McArthur was not with his troops during the final defensive battles in the Bataan Peninsula of the Phillipines in 1942. The General was ordered to withdraw, and he returned to fight another day.

General Sir Alexander MacDonald failed in his defensive preparations in Kintyre. His decisions after this, though, deserve to be viewed objectively. Splitting his retreating force and placing them in strong positions made as much sense as any other option available to him. It was clear to everyone on the ground on May 25 that Leslie's force was not going to be stopped in the field.

Sir James Turner hated Sir Alexander MacDonald, and this hatred coloured his account of events in Kintyre that May. This is not to say that his account is unreliable; far from it. He simply assumes the worst of Sir Alexander's intentions while reporting events accurately and honestly.

The actual defensive arrangements at Dunaverty are vague. Turner recorded that Sir Alexander had placed 300 men in a house on top of 'the hill called Dunaverty, environed with a stone wall on the one side, and the sea on the other, where there was not a drop of water but what fell from the clouds'. Interestingly he makes the same comment about the water situation at Dunaovaig Castle on Islay. He goes on to state that the garrison held out well until Leslie's troops stormed a trench at the foot of hill 'whereby they commanded two stripes of water'. The loss of this crucial water supply led eventually to a call for a parley.

Tradition has always suggested that on July 10 the besiegers discovered that the garrison's water was piped from a spring outside the walls to a well within. Having cut off this supply, and the weather becoming intensely hot, the garrison soon surrendered. The only eyewitness account (that of Sir James Turner), does not mention the pipes, and this has led to the story being discounted.

The actual site of Dunaverty even today helps in unravelling some of the above confusion. In the first place, the actual rock is far too small to accommodate anything like 300 men, so it seems likely that the fortress extended inland across the deep chasm described before and onto a raised mound overlooking Conieglen Water. The present course of this waterway dates back less than 200 years, therefore it is likely that the two stripes of water described by Turner were branches of it. This being the case Dunaverty's outer defences would have been at or near its water supply.

From sea level neither Dunaverty Rock nor the mound at its back appears particularly impressive. As they are approached, though, it becomes immediately apparent how difficult an assault would be. The mound is not high but it ripples with false tops and long ridges, which would be easily defended. Add walls (fixed or temporary) to these natural contours and it becomes easy to see why the Abhairtach first based themselves at this location.

Across the chasm from the mound is the rock itself, which is small but frighteningly steep. The remains of a structure can still be seen at the summit, but this position has to be a watchtower rather than a residence. The logic of a more extensive fortification becomes clearer from this vantage point. The highest point of the rock would have held the lookout position. Below this, on the western side, is a flat terrace suitable for an encampment. Further down, still to the west, would be the landing point for boats and a substantial modern jetty now occupies the position. The mound is to the north of the rock and extends onto the mainland, although a good part of it has sea along its eastern and western sides. The Old Statistical Account of Southend Parish describes several walls, one within the other, and this would be a logical defensive structure. There is enough evidence to show that the Fortress of Dunaverty extended inland beyond the simple basalt plug that is Dunaverty Rock.

Defensively, then, Dunaverty was impregnable. The traditional version of events states that Leslie's army attacked several times during June but were always beaten back with considerable losses. Direct force was not the answer but, as the wet and stormy weather that had featured throughout May gave way to dry and increasingly hot weather in June, the besiegers must have become aware of the importance of the water supply at the fortress's outer defences. From collecting water as it fell, the defenders now had to rely on the stream that ran past their stronghold.

Dunaverty Rock is a plug of dark basalt (not red sandstone as has been reported elsewhere), and this tough rock is not suitable for the digging of cisterns. As Sir James Turner rightly reported, the only water was what the heavens supplied, but, in Scotland, rain is such a regular visitor that thirst is not something the average Scotsman gives a great deal of thought to. Even as the weather grew hotter there was still the Conieglen Water and its two stripes defended by a substantial number of MacDonalds.

The story of the pipes leading into the defensive walls has to be given a little credence now. The image of MacDonald soldiers venturing out and drawing buckets of water under the rifles of the Covenanters is difficult to believe. A system drawing water from the river, through pipes and into the defences was practical, possible and sensible. So long as the arrangement was temporary the defenders had little to worry about.

Defensively Dunaverty is impregnable, but it has one weakness – water. As June became hotter and hotter Leslie saw his opportunity and ordered the Marquis of Argyle to launch a ferocious attack at the defensive point where the water supply was collected. Limiting the aims of the attack seems to have done the trick and Argyle's brigade killed 40 MacDonalds for only six losses on their own side. Was there a pipe? Was it cut? Was the position overrun? Whatever actually happened, Dunaverty was denied water. Only rain could save the garrison and, in defiance of Scotland's normal summer weather, none appeared and June just became hotter and drier.

General Leslie now secured his forward positions and waited. Faced with a quick death from thirst the defenders had little option other than to surrender. Their small numbers meant that an assault on Leslie's army would have been pointless. The traditional date of the surrender as being after July 10 has been convincingly refuted. It is likely that the actual date of the surrender was June 11, which means that the siege lasted not more than 10 or 11 days.

A total of 300 men walked out of Dunaverty into the hands of General Leslie. What followed next is one of the least known, yet most horrific incidents in Scottish history. The eyewitness account of Sir James Turner deserves to be fully quoted in this regard:

"We besieged Dunaverty, which kept out well enough till we stormed a trench they had at the foot of the hill, whereby they commanded two stripes of water. This we took, and in the assault, forty of them were put to the edge of the sword. We lost five or six, with Campbell of Skipness, Argyle's Major. After this inexecrable

thirst made them desire a parley. I was ordered to speak to them. Never could the Lieutenant-General be moved to grant any other conditions than that they should yield upon discretion or mercy: and it seemed strange to me to hear the Lieutenant-General's nice distinction, that they should yield themselves to the kingdom's mercy and not to his. At length they did so, and after they came out of the castle, they were put to the sword, every mother's son, except one young man MacKoull, whose life I begged, to be sent to France with one hundred country fellows whom we had smoked out of a cave, as they do foxes, and were given to Captain Campbell, the Chancellor's brother. Here it will be fit to make a stop till we canvas this cruel action. 1st: The Lieutenant-General was two days unresolved what to do with them. The Marquis of Argyle was accused, at his arraignment, for this murder, and I was examined as a witness. I declared that which was true, that I never heard him advise the Lieutenant-General to it. 2nd: Argyle was but a Colonel there, and so had no power to do it himself. 3rd: Tho' he had advised him to it, it was no capital crime, for counsel is no command. 4th: I several times spoke with the Lieutenant-General to save these mens' lives, and he always assented to it, and I know, of himself, he was unwilling to shed their blood. 5th: Mr John Nave who was appointed, by the Commissioners of the Kirk, to wait on him as Chaplain, never ceased to tempt him to that bloodshed, yea, and threatened him with the curses that befell Saul, for sparing the Amalekites, for with them his theology taught him to compare the Dunaverty men, and I verily believe this prevailed most with David Leslie, who looked on Nave as the representative of the Kirk of Scotland. Lastly, there is no doubt but the Lieutenant-General might well enough, without the least transgression of either custom, practice, law of war, or his Commission, to have used them as he did, for he was bound by no article to them, they having submitted themselves absolutely to his discretion. It is true, on the other hand, summum jus, summa injuria (the strict letter of the law is the greatest injustice): and in such cases, mercy is more Christian, the more honourable, and the more ordinary way in oour (sic) *wars in Europe: but really, I believe, advise him to that act who will, he hath repented it many times since, and even very soon after doing it."*

Local tradition says that the MacDonalds were bound together in twos and pushed off the eastern cliffs of the rock. There is no evidence of this, and Turner is open and honest enough about the massacre that we can rely on his mentioning such a thing had it occurred. There may be some symbolism in this legend, but the real events are horrifying enough without any additional embellishments. It is altogether more likely that, when Leslie had made his decision, he simply let his army loose on the captive garrison.

All manner of excuses can be made for this massacre: violent times, the extreme provocation of the MacDonalds during the preceding three years or General Leslie exercising his legalistic rights. Nothing carries any convincing justification. If this had been a simple clan dispute the modern reader needs only to look at the killed and maimed of Argyle and Lorne to excuse the Marquis of Argyle. If this had been a pitched battle then excesses are to be expected (if not applauded) on both sides. Neither of these excuses applies here. The dreadful tally of 300 prisoners were cold bloodedly butchered, but only after their captors, who were legally appointed officers of the kingdom, had held them for two days.

In February 1692, at Glencoe, 38 MacDonalds were killed by government soldiers who were Campbells. This massacre has resonated down through the centuries and is known around the world. The Campbell name has become synonymous with deceit and betrayal on account of Glencoe, where they accepted MacDonald hospitality for 10 days before turning on their hosts in the early hours of a bitter winter morning.

Numbers do not make one atrocity any more relevant than another. Dunaverty should not be remembered more passionately than Glencoe simply because 10 times as many MacDonalds died at the hands of Campbells. The unthinkable horror of keeping captives for two days before turning the army on them is certainly no worse than living as friends for 10 days and then throwing naked and injured women out into the snow to die.

The real horror of Dunaverty, and Glencoe, is not that one clan should have age old enmities with another. In both situations the Campbells were agents of the legitimate government of the time. The true horror is that any state should be so easily prepared to set aside the rule of law and instruct its agents to act with such reckless savagery.

It is good that Glencoe is remembered, and remembered for the correct reasons. What is regrettable is that it is remembered as a singular and unusual event; an aberration in the way the Scottish nation dealt with dissent. Dunaverty, 45 years earlier, should have been an early warning that Scotland, and then Britain, had a growing sense of where it intended to head. Dissent, whether political or religious, would be stamped out with extreme prejudice and, only later would the courts agonise over the rights and wrongs.

To this day, the Campbell name is viewed with distrust in many areas. I was informed by an acquaintance during the writing of this chapter that her family were MacDonalds. Her father was a GP during the 1940s, and this gentleman refused to ever treat a Campbell. All enquiries from persons of this name, or of associated clans, were referred to his partner.

In dealing with the massacre at Dunaverty, the name of Rev. John Nave has acquired notoriety far greater than any other leader who was there. Sir James Turner reported that he was the prime mover in demanding that the garrison be executed. His justification came from the Bible and First Samuel, where King Saul failed to carry out The Lord's explicit command to annihilate the Amelakites.

'Thus saith the Lord of hosts; I remember that which Amalek did to Israel, how he laid wait for him in the way, when he came up from Egypt. Now go and smite Amalek and utterly destroy all that they have, and spare them not; but slay both man and woman, infant and suckling, ox and sheep, camel and ass.

'And he took Agag the king of the Amalekites alive, and utterly destroyed all the people with the edge of the sword. But Saul and the people spared Agag, and the best of the sheep, and of the oxen, and of the fatlings, and the lambs, and all that was good, and would not utterly destroy them: but everything that was vile and refuse, that they destroyed utterly. Then came the word of the Lord unto Samuel, saying, It repenteth me that I have set up Saul to be king: for he is turned back from following me and hath not performed my commandments.

'...and Saul said unto him...I have performed the commandment of the Lord. And Samuel said, what meaneth then this bleating of the sheep in mine ears, and the lowing of the oxen which I hear?

'And Samuel said...For rebellion is as the sin of witchcraft, and stubbornness is as iniquity and idolatry. Because thou hast rejected the word of the Lord, he hath also rejected thee from being king...I will not return with thee...The Lord hath rent the Kingdom of Israel from thee this day.

'Then said Samuel, Bring ye hither to me Agag the king of the Amalekites. And Samuel hewed Agag in pieces before the Lord'....

Rev. Nave quoted repeatedly from this text, particularly 'what meaneth then this bleating of the sheep in mine ears, and the lowing of the oxen which I hear'? Fanaticism, pure and simple, and difficult for the 21st century mind to comprehend. General Leslie, though, and the Marquis of Argyle would have been less sure in their obvious tendency to mercy. Both were Covenanters, both were committed to the cause of Presbyterianism and both relied on Rev. Nave as the representative of the Kirk in their army.

There is no evidence to suggest that either the General or the Marquis were cruel men but what Rev. Nave was working on, undoubtedly in the belief that his position was correct, was their faith. Nave wholeheartedly believed that he was faced with a situation identical to that faced by Saul. He also believed that it was his task to remind both General Leslie and the Marquis of

Argyle that obedience to God will often involve doing things that are against your own instincts.

At Dunaverty something monstrous happened. To suggest, though, that those who initiated the massacre were, themselves, monsters is to impose the attitudes of the 21st century on those of the17th. If we return to Turner's testimony above we can glean a little of General Leslie's torment:

'…but really, I believe, advise him to that act who will, he hath repented it many times since, and even very soon after doing it'.

To his dying day, Leslie was torn between his own instinct for mercy and the clear and unambiguous demands of his faith. And Rev. Nave is only a monster if he acted as he did from motives of personal animosity to the Royalist Catholics at Dunaverty. Those true motives went with the reverend to his grave.

One exchange, reported between General Leslie and Rev. Nave, can be confidently dismissed. It was alleged at a later date that General Leslie, Argyle and Rev.Nave walked through the site of the massacre, ankle deep in blood. Leslie is said to have turned to Nave and said: "Now, Mr John, have you not for once got your full of blood?"

There is no spot at Dunaverty where any sort of liquid, far less blood, might lie to ankle depth on a day as hot as those June days in 1647. And quite why three senior officers would choose to stride through gore is something known only to one Bishop Guthrie, who first reported the above conversation.

Conclusion

The systematic way in which Dalriada and then Argyll have been removed from Scotland's official record is both fascinating and troubling. Fascinating because it highlights how unnecessary official censorship really is. All of the information in this book is readily available in libraries and on the Internet. There was also a vast resource of books about this area until the late 19th century. Today, outside Argyll, there is very little. No one ever stepped forward and ordered a book burning but what did happen was even more insidious.

As a child our lists of Kings and Queens always fascinated me. At some place in all encyclopaedias, large dictionaries and history books was a detailed list of Kings and Queens of England from 1066 until 1603, followed by a list of Kings and Queens of Great Britain from 1603 to the present. The implication was plain that in 1603 England had taken over Scotland and brought Anglo-Saxon civilisation to the north. As a committed Briton this view of the past suited me and I was seldom tempted to look into the matter any further.

In 1990 a political event occurred that prompted me to examine my Scottish roots more closely. The event was the introduction of the Poll Tax, and my concern, ironically, was not the tax itself; Governments levy taxes. Apart from lying, it is one of the things they routinely do. What concerned me most was something I remembered about the Act of Union that had united Scotland and England. No taxation was to be levied in Scotland unless it was *at the same time* levied in England. This particular issue was brought up in the House of Commons, but was quite sharply slapped down by the Speaker of the House.

As events slowly worked themselves out in protests and rioting in the streets I began to question just why the British Government would be doing this to one of its constituent nations. The answer that came was that the British Government had little regard for Scotland as anything other than an annexe to England. All of my life I had lived with my own image of Britain as the Union of England and Scotland, while the British Government regarded Britain and England as one and the same place with Scotland inconveniently tagged on somewhere up north.

A casual reference to encyclopaedias of the late 19th century paints a radically different picture of Great Britain. The compilers of these works clearly saw the Union in the same way that I did. Something changed this perception in the 20th century, and I have to confess that I am hard pressed to work out what it was. One defining moment, though, was the coronation of Queen Elizabeth. As monarch of the united realm her designation should have been simply Elizabeth, but it seems that Winston Churchill encouraged her to designate herself Elizabeth II, a plain and unmistakable insult to the Scots. A wander round any Scottish street to this day will uncover no Post Offices carrying the Queen's crest. Shortly after the coronation any crest carrying the E II R symbol was systematically blown up in Scotland. The authorities were quickly compelled to restore the crests of the Queen's father, George VI.

My faith in the idea of Great Britain remains undiminished, but my scorn for those who maliciously threw that idea to the wolves in 1990 will never leave me. As I turned from studying ancient Roman history and started to read up on my own history I was astounded to discover that, far from being an anglicised colony of our southern neighbour, most of the ideas surrounding Great Britain had originated in the north, not least the Royal dynasty that united the Crowns. Even to this day Britain is ruled at its heart by Scotsmen, many of whom have abandoned their Scots identity. At the time of writing, the Prime Minister is a Scotsman, Blair, although he would likely reject the idea. The Chancellor of the Exchequer is a Scotsman, Brown, who makes no pretence of his background and the Prime Minister's notorious former spin-doctor is a Scotsman, a Campbell no less.

So much for my fascination with the make-up of Great Britain. What troubled me was that the same process of creating a greater nation and then being forgotten by it seemed already to have happened to Dalriada. Was this the reason that Dalriada was never allowed to be taught about in Scottish schools? Of course this would imply a direct approach to confusing the Scots and their sense of their own history. Much better and more insidious to simply divert them down wrong paths.

As a child I loved tales about King Harold 11's valiant defence at Stamford Bridge, followed by his exhausted defeat at Hastings. All through my childhood the schools gave me a well-deserved respect for the history of the English people and their heroes. A daytrip to the Bannockburn exhibition near Stirling did little to divert the English orientation of my teaching. I did not have a clue who King Robert was and quite why this 'little' battle was so pathetically significant. It never once occurred to me to question why a Scotsman was being taught so much English history.

So the question I close this work with is: If Dalriada could give Scotland its initial sense of nationhood and identity and then be forgotten, what is the likelihood that Scotland, which gave its monarchy to Great Britain and then supported the union with passion, might suffer the same fate? The job is already half completed. In general we are a nation with little sense of our own history or importance. The last thing that galvanised any sense of Scottishness was the movie *Braveheart,* which was, in truth, a stirring but miserably inaccurate adventure story.

The subsequent creation of a Scottish Parliament has, if anything made the Scots more cynical about their history and their sense of independence. Given an unrivalled opportunity to become the founding fathers of a resurgent nation, some Members of the Scottish Parliament have already shown themselves to be, at worst, unreliable politicians and, at best, fifth rate civil servants.

It may turn out that the British state has had the last laugh on Scotland by giving it what it thought it wanted. I sincerely hope that this proves not to be the case. What Britain will perhaps never understand is that without Scotland it is nothing, not even a Greater England.

Perhaps this is a lesson from Dalriada as well, for without its Celtic heritage Scotland would, indeed, have become just North England.

Bibliography

Donald Gregory — *The History of the Western Highlands and Islands of Scotland AD 1493-1625*

Mike Ashley — *The Mammoth Book of British Kings and Queens*

Nigel Tranter — *The Story of Scotland*
Norman S Newton — *Campbeltown's Churches*
Angus Martin — *Kintyre: The Hidden Past*
Simon Schama — *A History of Britain*
S A Handford — *Caesar: The Conquest of Gaul*
Dr Charles Hase — *A History of the Christian Church*
Neil Grant — *The Campbells of Argyll*
J Mac Master Campbell — *The Story of Gigha*
Freddy Gillies — *The Viking Isle*
E William Robertson — *Scotland Under Her Early Kings*
James A Robertson — *The Gael of Alban*
Mary McGrigor — *Argyll:Land of Blood and Beauty*
Terry Deary — *Horrible Histories: Ireland*
The Bible (King James Version)
The Dunaverty Massacre 1776

I would also like to thank everyone who, by various means, helped me in the compilation of this book. This invaluable assistance was very much appreciated, and it was also encouraging to discover along the way that so many people in Argyll remain fascinated by their own history. I won't list these friends; you know who you are. Thank you. BJ

Printed in Great Britain by CPI Bath